Problem Regions of Europe
General Editor: **D. I. Scargill**

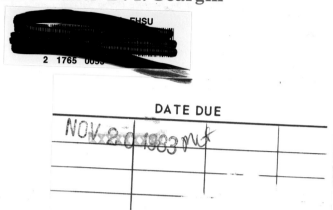
The Eastern Alps

Elisabeth Lichtenberger

Oxford University Press 1975

Oxford University Press, Ely House, London W.1

Glasgow New York Toronto Melbourne Wellington
Cape Town Ibadan Nairobi Dar es Salaam Lusaka Addis Ababa
Delhi Bombay Calcutta Madras Karachi Lahore Dacca
Kuala Lumpur Singapore Hong Kong Tokyo

© Oxford University Press 1975

Filmset by BAS Printers Limited, Wallop, Hampshire
and printed in Great Britain
at the University Press, Oxford
by Vivian Ridler, Printer to the University

Editor's Preface

Great economic and social changes have taken place in Europe in recent years. The agricultural workforce in the west was halved, for example, during the 1950s and 1960s. This unprecedented flight from the land has made possible some much-needed reorganization of farm holdings but it has also created problems, not least that of finding uses for land in the highlands and elsewhere where it is no longer profitable to farm. Closely related is the difficulty of maintaining services to a much diminished rural population or of providing new kinds of services for the holidaymakers who increasingly buy up rural properties.

Contraction of the labour force has also taken place in many traditional industries. The coal-mining industry alone has shed two-thirds of its workforce since 1950. The resulting problems have been especially serious in those mining or manufacturing districts which have a high level of dependence on a single source of employment—a not uncommon result of Europe's industrial past—and the efforts of those who seek to attract new industries are often thwarted by a legacy of pollution, bad housing, and soured labour relations.

Quite a different set of problems has arisen in the great cities of Europe such as London and Paris and in the conurbations of closely linked cities well exemplified by Randstad Holland. Here are problems due to growth brought about by the expansion of consumer-orientated manufacturing and still more by the massive increase in office jobs which proliferate in 'down-town' business districts. The problems are economic, social and political, and they include the effects of congestion, of soaring land values, of the increasing divorce of place of residence from place of work, and of the difficulty of planning a metropolitan region that may be shared between many independent-minded local authorities.

The problems resulting from change are not passing ones; indeed they exhibit a persistence that amply justifies their study on an areal basis. Hence the *Problem Regions of Europe* series. The volumes in the series have all been written by geographers who, by the nature of their discipline, can take a broadly based approach to description and analysis. Geographers in the past have been reluctant to base their studies on problem regions since the problem was often of a temporary nature, less enduring than the 'personality' of the region but the magnitude of present-day problems has even resulted in the suggestion that regions should be defined in terms of the problems that confront them.

Certain themes emerge clearly when the basis of the problem is examined: the effects of a harsh environment, of remoteness and of political division, as well as of industrial decay or urban congestion. But these have not been examined in isolation and the studies that make up the series have been carefully chosen in order that useful comparisons can be made. Thus, for example, both the Mezzogiorno and Andalusia have to contend with the problems of Mediterranean drought, wind, and flood, but the precise nature of these and other problems, as well as man's response to them, differs in the two regions. Similarly, the response to economic change is not the same in North-East England as in North Rhine–Westphalia, nor the response to social pressures the same in Paris as in the Randstad.

The efforts which individual governments have made to grapple with their problems provides a basis for critical assessment in each of the volumes. For too long, solutions were sought that were piecemeal and short-term. Our own Development Areas in Britain provide a good illustration of this kind of policy. Of late, however, European governments have shown an increasing awareness of the need to undertake planning on a regional basis. The success or otherwise of such regional policies is fully explored in the individual *Problem Region* volumes.

When it was first planned the *Problem Region* series was thought of as useful only to the sixth-form student of geography. As it has developed it has become clear that the authors—all specialists in the geography of the areas concerned—have contributed studies that will be useful, not only for sixth-form work, but as a basis for the more detailed investigations undertaken by advanced students, both of geography and of European studies in general.

D.I.S.

St. Edmund Hall, Oxford

3

Contents

page

Introduction 5

1 The Crisis of Mountain Farming 7
Background 7
Reasons for depopulation 9
   Unfavourable environmental conditions 9
   Social structures 11
   Economic causes 13
Consequences of depopulation 14
   Zuhuben 14
   Forsthuben 14
The extent of change 15
The effect on the Alpine economy 17
The rise of forestry and hunting 21

2 Readjustment of the Mountain Peasantry 23
Self-aid measures 23
Extra sources of income 24
Public aid 25
   Price policy measures 25
   Subsidies and credit 26

3 Tourism and Recreation 29
The Eastern Alps: a region of transit 29
The growth of tourism 30
Trends in tourism 31
Importance of tourism 32
Factors favouring tourism 33
   Environmental attractions 33
   Existing settlements 34
   Personal factors 34
Buildings 35
Extent of tourism 36
The concentration problem 36
   Regional concentration 36
   Seasonal concentration 37
   Concentration by nationality 37
Peasants and tourists 38
Public aid for tourism 39
Problems posed by tourism 40
   Natural hazards 40
   Management problems 40
   Social problems 41

4 Problems in their Subregional Context 42
Perspectives of mass tourism 42
   Summer and winter visitors 42
   Recreation for city-dwellers 43
The areas of mountain peasantry 45
Strategy for the future 46

Further Work 48

Introduction

The nature of the problems

Of late years there has been a fundamental change in the evaluation of the Alps. The former preserve of the mountain peasantry has become the recreation area of an urban population. Change has not taken place everywhere to the same extent, however. It has varied according to differences in the physical qualities of the areas, their socio-economic make-up, and the different planning objectives of the countries involved.

The concept of the Alps as a potential recreation area for urbanized Western and Central Europe has not been universally accepted so far. There are influential people who advocate the preservation of mountain farming by suitable political measures. Opinions differ widely in the countries concerned, namely Austria, Germany, Italy, and Switzerland.

From the facts mentioned above it can be seen that there are two sides to the problem. On the one hand, the traditional way of life of mountain peasants and their economic activities cannot be adapted easily to the new conditions of an industrial era. Agriculture has become increasingly concentrated in areas suited to mechanization and to intensive cropping. In less-favoured regions, land has been abandoned and loss of population has taken place from settlements over vast areas. In this way the longstanding balance between mountain pasture and valley settlement has been broken. Change has taken two forms. First, mountain pastures in the higher regions have been drastically diminished, to an even greater extent than the actual settlements. Secondly, as to the lower regions, the settlements in the valleys have lost their hinterland and, therefore, a great deal of their economic basis. The extent of this development differs widely in the various regions and deserves more detailed discussion.

On the other hand, the Eastern Alps have acquired new functions and gained higher value by tourist traffic. Tourism has not extended to all regions, and in some parts it has not taken advantage of existing rural settlements. There are areas, however, in which the rural population has taken the initiative and succeeded in gaining a foothold in the tourist industry.

The needs of tourists have led to the construction of roads which in turn has encouraged the growth of industry in the valleys and the building of houses by the resident population. But tourist traffic has also had negative effects on agriculture, and it is apparent that it cannot be absorbed in the way some political experts in the field of agriculture thought it could be.

The causes of the problems

A deeper insight into the problems can be gained only from a study of the historical background. Changes, such as the loss of pack-horse transport and of charcoal-burning during the industrial revolution, must be taken into account, as well as the effect of the iron industry in the first half of the 19th century, of gentlemen-hunters in the second half of the century, later on of paper-mills, and, at present, of enterprises in the timber industry.

Cattle rearing, the traditional occupation in the mountainous areas, experienced a serious setback when it was intensified in the Alpine forelands. Environmental disadvantages made themselves felt even more when mechanization was adopted. The influence of other factors was responsible for regional variations in the extent of change: the nature of land ownership, ethnic contrasts, different economic links with the lowlands, and political intervention of the respective governments in agricultural matters.

From the turn of the century tourist traffic appeared on the scene. Until World War I it was completely separated from the established rural settlements and their economic activities. Since that time it has become, in some areas at least, an increasingly significant influence. Like industry, it tends to be a concentrated activity. Thus it quickly upsets any balance which might otherwise be reached between it and agriculture.

The planning strategies

Fairly early, political experts in the field of agriculture showed their interest in the problems of mountain farming. Since the inter-war period there have been various programmes under the collective title of 'Aid to Mountain Peasants'. Opinions of the functions of mountain agriculture and, therefore, of the type and extent of protection and subsidies, vary in the respective countries. They also change as governments come and go. Some of the countries, such as Austria, allow special tax reductions to mountain-farming villages.

Newly developed winter-sports area on the Turrach Lake, Carinthia (Austria)

As the influence of the European Common Market increases, the verdict of its experts on agriculture is heard more frequently. They do not believe mountain farming can survive. The farmers are to be considered landscape conservationists, to be paid for by tourist traffic. More recently proponents of various kinds of tourist traffic have made their influence felt in the region of high mountain chains where they have invested outside funds. There are not as yet laws preventing the building of holiday homes for the urban population of neighbouring countries who do not contribute by paying taxes towards an improvement to the services or to the conservation of the landscape.

The favourable outward appearance of well-kept tourist centres effectively hides the enormous debts that made the improvements possible. A decline in tourist traffic would be catastrophic for the majority of the tourist centres in the Alps. Furthermore, there is as yet no uniform view of the future development of the Alps. Various strategies are being discussed:

1. for agriculture, the forming of rural co-operatives, plus an improvement of the services offered (especially to scattered settlements in mountainous areas), for example roads, medical services of all types, and school buses for the children;

2. afforestation, organized by public authorities in extensively farmed areas;

3. the spreading of tourist traffic over larger areas and the involvement of all regions as far as possible; and

4. an increase in industrial activities in the large Alpine valleys, with commuters travelling from the higher regions.

1 The Crisis of Mountain Farming

Background

The difficulties faced by agriculture in the process of adjustment to industrialization is a recurring theme of all studies relating to the countryside. A decrease of rural population and in the number of farm holdings is a common feature of such development. To some extent, its effects can be offset by rationalization, mechanization, and specialization in the physically more-favoured lowlands. The efficiency of even the upland farms can be increased. Circumstances are different in the Alps however. There is a more fundamental type of rural exodus to be observed—a permanent drift of the population towards lower-lying regions, necessarily involving a complete change of land-use and the total abandonment of some settlements. In the Alpine States the public first became aware of this process during the last third of the nineteenth century. At that time a large number of farms in Eastern Austria were acquired for use as hunting lodges.

Economists and administrators have led the way in the ensuing discussions against a changing political background. The points of view taken range from, on the one hand, a romantic glorification of the mountain peasantry seen as the ethically and biologically most valuable element of the population to, on the other hand, the depiction of a marginal group for whom there is no room in the E.E.C. The latter is the view of Sicco Mansholt, a leading European expert in agricultural politics.

Both of these extreme views need to be revised. Generally speaking, all discussions of the problem of mountain peasantry are encumbered by preconceived notions that need to be dispelled.

It is only partly true, for example, to say that the high mountainous areas constitute a natural source of population for urbanization and industrialization. These areas have a slow rate of population growth, for which there are several reasons. The average age of marriage has always been very high, and the percentage of married people has remained low. Furthermore, infant mortality has been high, whilst the number of births per couple has been comparatively small. Thus there never was a surplus of population of more than 10 to 15 per cent, in marked contrast with the lowlands of eastern Central Europe (Poland, Hungary, Romania, etc.) which had a ready surplus of agricultural population.

During the present century the emigration of younger age groups has accelerated, bringing about a rapid decrease of population in the high mountainous regions and leaving a predominance of elderly people. As even girls living in the country are not willing to marry the heirs of farms high up in the mountains, there is a noticeable surplus of men in the older age groups. The proportion of married people has therefore remained low. As compared with the development in towns, mountain families, generally speaking, are still made up of three generations, and there are only a few small households comprising a married couple and their (one or two) children. The reduction of the population did not destroy the old patriarchal structures completely, but rather undermined them. Very complicated and fragmented households came into existence. Examples can be found of distant relatives, male or female, jointly running a farm. In addition to these holdings without a proper heir, there are still farms managed by families with many children, five or six or even more. Their number is, however, everywhere decreasing in the Eastern Alps. Closest to the towns, contacts with an urban way of life have brought about a pronounced tendency to exercise birth control.

Some political economists maintain that the crisis of the mountain peasantry was brought about by the transition from a traditional self-sufficient economy to a market-oriented one. Their view is based mainly on the fact that the mountain peasants used to grow their own grain for making bread even at a considerable height above sea level. This, however, was no more true in the past than it is now. On looking back to the period when the forests of the Alps were cleared, we find that as early as the twelfth century the mountainous areas provided a surplus of cattle for the flourishing towns of the northern and southern forelands. Up to the eighteenth century the leasing of the oxen trade (from Carinthia to Italy) to Italian merchants constituted one of the major sources of income of the Crown. Today the need to export the produce of the mountain farmers, namely milk, butter, and cheese, cattle and timber, is still one of the specific economic problems of the two most wholly Alpine countries: Austria and Switzerland.

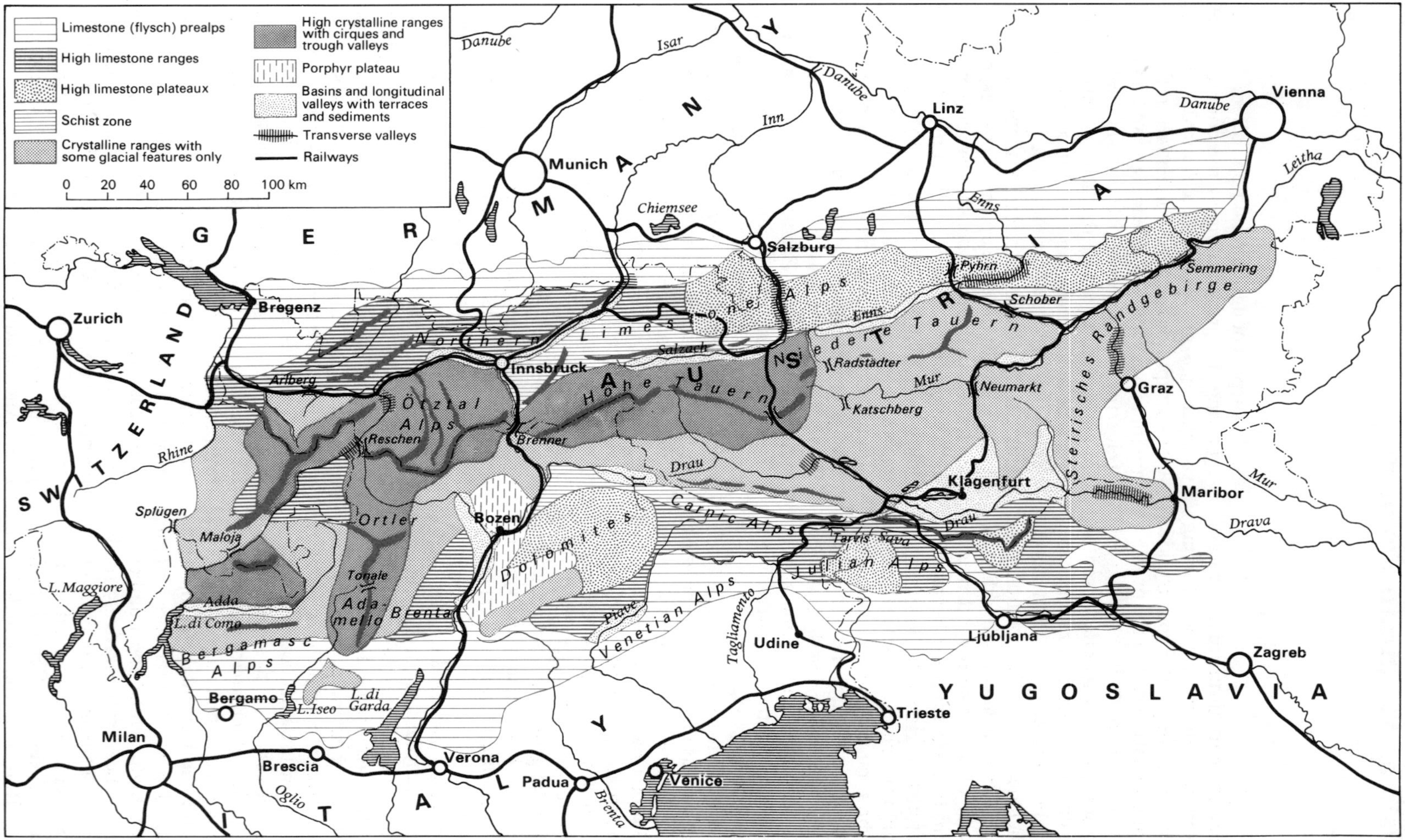

Map 1. Physiography of the Eastern Alps

8

Also contrary to the idea of self-sufficiency is the fact that some sort of extra, non-agricultural income has provided a substantial share of the livelihood of the mountain peasants ever since the extension of farming into the high mountain regions took place during the Middle Ages. These sources of extra income have taken different forms over the course of the centuries, and their profitability or otherwise has greatly influenced the prosperity of the mountain settlements to the present day. During the Middle Ages of greatest importance were mining and carting; later on charcoal-burning and cottage industry; and nowadays tourism and industry in the valleys are providing employment.

Another fact that must be established at the outset is that agricultural holdings are not of uniform size. There are distinct differences which are closely related to the traditional forms of inheritance and the degree of division which this involves.

To be precise, the term 'mountain peasant' (*Bergbauer*) should be applied only in areas where the inheritance is not divided, namely the Bavarian Alps, the greater part of the Austrian Alps, and the Southern Tyrol. In those areas where there is equal division of property amongst the heirs—western Tyrol and Vorarlberg in Austria as well as the Swiss and Italian Alps—the term 'mountain cottager' (*Bergkeuschler*) should be used. Where it took place, the continuous fragmentation of holdings resulted at an early date in units that could not survive without some sort of extra income and seasonal migration. Thus, the problems of the mountain farmers are quite different in these two areas of dissimilar forms of inheritance.

In addition, there are differences with regard to ownership which accentuate the contrasts. In those areas where the inheritances are not divided, the peasants themselves are the owners of the land; whereas various forms of leasing and, therefore, non-resident urban proprietors are of great importance in the Italian Alps where inheritances are divided equally. By contrast, the small and miniature holdings of the Swiss and western Austrian Alps are predominantly owned by the peasants.

It was noted above that the abandonment of settlements in the Alps was not a phenomenon of the industrial revolution but had begun much earlier. The apex of mountain agriculture had been reached late in the Middle Ages, when mining and carting flourished and there were many additional jobs in mines and salt-works. After that the upper limit of permanent rural settle-

TABLE I

The percentage distribution of farm sizes in the Alps

| | Hectares of cultivated land | | | |
	up to 5	5–10	10–20	over 20
West Germany	39·6	44·5		15·9
Austria	31·4	34·8		33·8
Italy	81·7	10·8	3·9	3·6
Switzerland	51·8	25·7	19·1	3·4

ments continued to decline, sometimes slowly and in a localized fashion, sometimes more quickly and over larger areas. This trend was, to a large extent, influenced by the economic prosperity of the non-rural settlements in the interior basins and the Alpine forelands. It was here that an economic crisis related to changes in feudal organization initiated the first phase of drift from the high mountainous areas. At the same time mining in the mountains became less profitable, and the old bridle-paths fell into disuse. When the new roads were built during the eighteenth century, settlements in the low-lying areas with access to long-distance trade routes gained an additional advantage over those at high elevations. Not only were the latter situated far away from any transport, but they also lost their income derived from the carrying trade. This resulted in a continuing contraction of settlements at high levels.

The decisive blow to settlements in the high mountains, however, came with the *Grundentlastung* of 1848 which terminated the manorial system. The holdings of the mountain peasants were drawn into the whirlpool of international economics, becoming subject to the rules of and regulation of prices by a capitalistic real-estate market and affected by the creation of new wage levels in industry. From this time onwards, during the so-called 'Founders' Period' (1840–1918), the rural exodus was bound up with urbanization and expansion of industry, not only in the Alpine forelands but in the basins and wide longitudinal valleys within the Alps themselves.

Reasons for depopulation
Unfavourable environmental conditions
Unfavourable environmental conditions in mountainous areas are brought about by different agents which vary in importance from place to place. Depopulation is undoubtedly greater on slopes in the shade, where, for example, the growing season is shortened by about three weeks at a height of 1500 m in the Central Alps. Contrasts between the northern and southern slopes of the Alpine valleys, although always a noticeable effect in the Eastern Alps with regard to the upper

limit and density of settlements, have increased in significance since the last century: the slopes facing north have been deserted over large tracts.

On the other hand, it has been shown in the Tyrol that the effect of landslides and avalanches on the disappearance of farmsteads has been greatly over-estimated. Buildings destroyed by disasters of this type are normally re-erected somewhere else.

Slope, however, seems to be an important factor, and different measures have been undertaken to overcome its associated problems. Ingeniously constructed stone terraces are to be found even at great heights in the Italian Alps; but they are missing in the Austrian and German Alps, where, as long as the fields were tilled (that is, until World War II), the soil that was washed downwards had to be carried upwards again, normally in baskets. In the Tyrol even children could be seen doing this hard work until quite recently.

Modernized agriculture in the Eastern Alps concentrates on the production of fodder nowadays, as crop farming is losing importance. Slope sets a limit in this connection also. At a gradient of 25 to 30 per cent, small furrows (parallel to the contours) start forming when cattle graze there. In this way the turf is broken and soil erosion sets in. On slopes of 25 per cent tractors can still be used, whilst mowers and winches help to utilize even steeper slopes (up to about 45 degrees) as meadows. Steeper slopes can be mowed only with scythes. An angle of 70 degrees constitutes the limit for grazing. Formerly hay (*Wildheu*, 'hay on the rocks') was produced there with the aid of crampons and sickles, but most of these *Bergmähder* are no longer used today.

Exposure and slope determine the profitability of agriculture in the high mountains and thereby exercise a high degree of control on the distribution of settlement, both of individual farmsteads and of villages. But relief features do not operate alone; and account must also be taken of accessibility, which factor has counted most in time of economic crisis. Disadvantages are greatest for scattered settlements in the highly dissected crystalline mountains with their gorges and V-shaped valleys in eastern Austria and amongst the ridges lying between the main valleys of the Central and Southern Alps. When settlements on a lower level are being deserted, all the farmsteads higher up normally follow. It has been possible to retain chains of settlement in valleys high up in the mountains if traffic has not been impeded by steep, gorgelike stretches at the mouth of the valley, a feature characteristic of the Southern Alps.

The problem of inaccessibility has been reduced as new roads have been built and the motor vehicle has come into wider use. Since World War II, for example, 70 000 km of approach roads have been constructed in Austria with the help of public funds. The amount of investment in this field differs widely from country to country, however.

A reader not well versed in Alpine conditions might wonder why absolute height has not yet been mentioned. It is, in fact, of remarkably little over-all importance in the Eastern Alps because of the enormous variety of physical conditions found there, and it might even give a false impression if used as a guideline.

Of far greater significance than altitude alone is the location of the settlements in relation to the zones of natural vegetation. These zones are the best clue to the value of the site, setting limits to potential forms of land use. Figs. 1 and 2 are

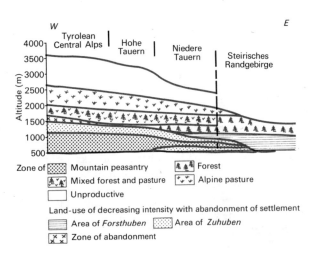

Fig. 1. Profile of the Austrian Central Alps from west to east showing settlement and land-use associated with the mountain peasantry

intended to give an impression of the great environmental differences to be observed within the Eastern Alps.

The schematic profile (Fig. 1) along the main crest of the crystalline Central Alps in Austria, from the Tyrol to the eastern versant in Styria, illustrates the gradual decline of all of the upper limits. The summit heights decline most rapidly: they reach 3800 m in the Tyrol, are only about 2800 m in the *Niedere Tauern* in Styria, and do not exceed 1800–2200 m in the *Steirisches Randgebirge*. The timber-line is found at about 2200 m in the west and at 1800 m in the east. In the west, therefore, there is room for a zone of Alpine pastures extending for about 500 m below a largely glaciated area of barren land. The upper limit of permanent settlement declines much more rapidly from west to east. It lies at 1900 m in the valleys high up in the Tyrolean Central Alps, but at only about 1000 m in the east.

In this schematic profile the upper limit of land-use by the mountain peasants is indicated and a distinction made between two types involving forestry: the *Waldbauern* in the east and the *Almbauern* (summer ranches) in the west. Study shows that the existence of these two types is being endangered in different ways. It is surprising that it is not so much in the west, where man is defending a kind of pioneer frontier against wilderness and barren land, that the number of peasant holdings is declining, but in the forest mountains to the east. There, the mountain peasantry is experiencing a crisis from the uppermost limit of settlement right down to the valley floors. Environmental conditions cannot explain this phenomenon. It can be understood only against the background of the social system as a whole, a subject which is examined below.

Whereas the profile from west to east illustrates the decline of all the upper limits, the profile drawn from north to south (Fig. 2) represents the Alps as a divide between the Central European and Mediterranean climatic regions. Submediterranean plant types push northwards from the Po valley into the large valleys of (from west to east) the Adda, Aglio, Adige, Brenta, and Tagliamento. Here is intensive culture of the vine and other fruits with associated irrigation. The effect is to push the zone of mountain peasantry to a higher level. It follows that this often involves an even more precarious existence than that to be found on the northern slope of the Eastern Alps. There, only gradual differences, both with regard to agriculture and to the way of life, can be observed between the peasants of the mountains and those of the valleys.

Moreover the destruction of forests, encouraged by torrential Mediterranean rains but initiated by gross misuse of the communal woodland, robbed the majority of rural holdings in the Southern Italian Alps of a source of capital. Forests are very important to the peasants in the North-eastern Alps, where individual ownership and the example set by business magnates and the nobility who owned large tracts of forest resulted in carefully planned exploitation. Deciduous forests are predominant in the Southern Alps. Most of them, however, have been turned into stunted coppices, no longer providing anything but fuel for local use.

Social structures

In the introduction it was pointed out that two fundamentally different social systems meet in the Eastern Alps. First, peasants, proud of their fairly extensive possessions and living in scattered settlements, are characteristic mainly of the German and Austrian Alps. Secondly, peasants

Fig. 2. Profile of the mountain peasants' settlements and land-use along the longitude of Innsbruck

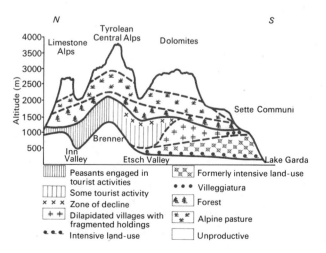

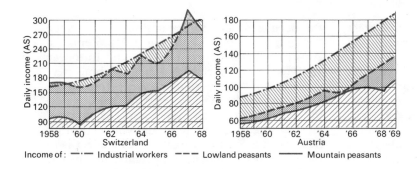

Fig. 3. Disparity of income between mountain and lowland peasants and industrial workers in Switzerland and in Austria (1958–1968/9)

Income of: —·— Industrial workers – – – Lowland peasants —— Mountain peasants

and tenants working tiny holdings and preferring to live in nucleated settlements are predominant in the Italian Alps.

The significance of social conditions will be considered first in relation to the German and Austrian Alps. Although larger holdings predominate here, in discussing the desertion of farmsteads, it is mainly the small holdings (under 20 hectares) possessing little woodland that are being reduced in number. They correspond with family enterprises that are no longer viable under present economic conditions. On the other hand many fairly large and well-equipped farms (100 hectares and more) have been abandoned also. They have fallen victims to the problems arising from the shortage and cost of farm-hands or from the demands of potential buyers.

There have been and still are two main groups of buyers of mountain farms in the German and Austrian Alps. One is the well-to-do peasants of the valleys who are interested in buying farmsteads high up in the mountains in order to use those areas as pastures. This kind of holding (*Zuhuben*) now plays an important role in the settlement pattern and economy in the Tyrol, in Salzburg, and in Carinthia. In addition, there have been large groups of non-rural buyers. Whereas rural buyers were concerned mainly with enlarging the area suitable for grazing and fodder production, non-rural buyers aimed initially at exploiting the forests. As early as the eighteenth century the owners of hammer mills in iron-making districts of Styria and Carinthia were buying rural properties. In this way they tried to secure the increasing amounts of charcoal required by their industry.

During the late nineteenth century a new group of purchasers emerged, consisting of industrial entrepreneurs, bankers, and lawyers—some of them, in imitation of feudal traditions, wanting to acquire hunting grounds of their own, the others looking for secure investment after the disastrous commercial crisis of 1873. During the inter-war period they were joined by timber merchants and pulp and paper companies anxious to secure their supply of raw materials, as the owners of hammer mills had been almost 200 years earlier. Recently, new urban groups have joined the interested parties. They hope to acquire apartments for weekend and holiday use and are, therefore, interested in the buildings more than in the lands surrounding them.

The role of ethnic groups should be mentioned at this point. Some of them tend more than others to retain a firm hold on their rural properties. Southern Tyrol can serve as a model in this respect. There the opposition of German-speaking peasants to the towns Italianized by industrialization has served to build up a sort of barrier against rural exodus. Only as national enmities have started disappearing among the younger generation has this barrier been gradually removed. An increasing number of farmsteads in the Southern Tyrol are thus deserted today.

The villages high in the mountains of the Italian Alps are characterized by tiny holdings fragmented as a result of the equal division of inherited property. Their multi-storey buildings have an urban appearance and are always inhabited by several families, differing markedly from the various types of farmhouse in those parts of the Alps where the holdings are not divided. Seasonal migration always has been, and still is, an inseparable part of the life of these Italian mountain farms, fragmented over the course of many centuries. It should be noted that it was only the arable land that was split up. Pastures and coppices degraded by grazing and hunting remained communal property. Agriculture could not provide an economic basis for the growing population which was therefore reduced by large-scale emigration to the United States, both before and after World War I. Reduction of the population in this way and the disappearance of many small enterprises resulted in the disorganization of many activities traditionally carried out on a community basis. The first to be affected was the supervision of the complicated forms of irrigation, necessary because of the dry summers.

Terraces, characteristic of the areas of *cultura mixta* in the Mediterranean, had been introduced in these higher regions, where they had proved useful in reducing soil erosion at a time when only manual labour was used. Nowadays they impede mechanization both of arable farming and in the utilization of meadows. They are one of the main reasons for the more extensive nature of farming over large parts of the cultivated areas of the Italian Alps. Where they are missing, for example, in the Brescia forealps (Val Trampia), intensive use of the meadows has been retained even on steepest slopes.

Little property has been sold to outside purchasers in this part of the Alps. Most of the emigrants did not sell their property, but let it lie fallow. Recently afforestation of tiny lots has begun. In these villages high in the mountains a once extremely sophisticated system of cultivation, requiring a great deal of labour, would seem to have little future. There is no obvious solution to the problem.

Economic causes

Statistics illustrating the disparity of incomes between agriculture and industry are available for Switzerland and Austria (Fig. 3), showing marked differences between these two States. There is no country attaching more importance than Switzerland to the income of the peasants and their families in determining the prices of the agricultural produce. Farm income is, so to speak, determined officially and is kept as high as that of qualified workers in industry. The increase in farm income between 1958 and 1968 was not only a consequence of higher yields due to rationalization, but also of a large increase in commodity prices. In Austria, by contrast, the disparity between the wages of industrial workers and the income of the peasants more than doubled over the same period.

Fig. 3 also illustrates the gap in incomes between the enterprises in the valleys and those high in the mountains. Both in Switzerland and in Austria the mountain peasants are clearly underprivileged, reaching only 60 per cent of the average income. It should be noted, however, that the difference between the two types of enterprise is much smaller in Austria than in Switzerland. The position of Swiss mountain peasants is thus more marginal than that of the Austrian ones, since they are worse off than all other groups of the population including the peasants of the valleys.

In Austria, this problem is only one among many others in the field of agriculture. On the other hand the diagram helps to explain why so much importance is attached to public aid for the mountain peasants in Switzerland. A fundamental economic and organizational problem (Fig. 4) forms the background to this disparity of incomes between enterprises in the low-lying areas and those situated high up. The enlargement of holdings allows for mechanization and brings about improvements in the low-lying areas since it involves a higher *per capita* income, but it does not have a similar effect in the high mountainous regions. Unfavourable conditions caused by the relief may result in a lowering of the *per capita* income, even though a larger area is being farmed.

A higher income can be earned only from the sale of timber, and there is no point in enlarging holdings unless forested areas are added. These are a valuable support to many mountain peasants, a kind of savings bank which they can rely on when larger investments are necessary, for example, when machines are bought or a house is built. The larger farms have begun to adopt this solution. First, they reduce the cultivated area, it being too large for the labour available, and then they make more intensive use of the flatter ground near the house. The steeper slopes with an inclination of 20 to 40 per cent (where mechaniza-

Fig. 4. Size of holdings and income per hectare of mountain and foreland peasants in Austria

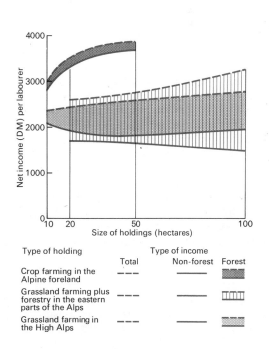

Type of holding	Total	Type of income	
		Non-forest	Forest
Crop farming in the Alpine foreland	- - -	———	(dark shading)
Grassland farming plus forestry in the eastern parts of the Alps	- - -	———	(vertical hatch)
Grassland farming in the High Alps	- - -	———	(diagonal hatch)

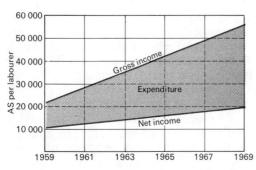

Fig. 5. The widening gap between gross and net incomes of agricultural holdings in the Austrian Alps

tion is difficult), shady slopes, and even steeper and rocky areas are afforested.

Although yields are still being increased in the mountains, the prices obtained for farm products have not kept up with those paid for equipment, seed, fertilizers, etc. Thus, expenditure has increased faster than income (Fig. 5). In consequence, it does not pay, for example, to have a new, modern stable built, as a loan to meet the high construction costs will be necessary. Income derived from cattle breeding will be lower than when the old byre is being used. Often it does not pay to buy machinery even though it could be used on steep slopes; it can be utilized profitably only when the lots have a certain minimum size which can rarely be attained because of the relief.

Consequences of depopulation

Following depopulation, certain changes take place in the land-use and settlement of the Eastern Alps. It is possible to categorize these changes under a number of headings. In the area of scattered settlements where holdings are not subdivided (Austria, Germany, Southern Tyrol) there are two types of 'successor holdings': first, the so-called *Zuhube*, where an additional farm is normally acquired by a peasant, and secondly, the so-called *Forsthube*, where the change has resulted from the intrusion of a non-rural population.

Zuhuben (second farms)

In the eastern Austrian Alps two sub-types are to be found: the *Zuhube* proper and the *Halthube*. Both originated from a desire to increase the agricultural potential of the main holding. On the *Zuhube*, meadows are utilized and there is even a certain amount of arable land, whereas there are only pastures on the *Halthube*. The outward appearance of *Zuhube* buildings does not differ greatly from that of ordinary farmhouses, though they are likely to be much older. They may be

inhabited by people owning no land (*Inwohner*)—these tend in most cases to be road-makers or woodcutters—or by a *Moar*, an individual or a family looking after the farmer's cattle and keeping his house in good repair. Usually the wages of a *Moar* are fairly low, but he is entitled to cultivate arable land and to graze his own stock (goats or one or two cows). When the *Zuhube* is situated next to the farmstead, the older buildings may be demolished and the lots united with those of the main holding. This system of land-use on *Zuhuben* was quite common in the second half of the nineteenth century. Since World War II it has been disappearing as it gets increasingly difficult for the peasants to find suitable *Moars*.

Unlike the *Zuhuben* on which land-use may be intensified, the *Halthube* represents a first step towards a more extensive use of the land. Originally it was intended to provide extra pastures and forage crops for an increased number of stock. Because of the shortage of labour, however, the meadows are no longer mowed and are used only as permanent pastures. The house is not inhabited, dilapidation sets in, and it may even be demolished. As little care is taken of the pastures, especially when the distance between the main farmstead and the acquired *Halthube* is great, scrub and trees begin to grow and eventually even the stable or shed goes to ruin.

This gradual extension of land-use is a characteristic feature nowadays even in those areas of the mountains where *Zuhuben* have predominated. There is really only one long-term solution to the difficulty: the *Halthuben* must be afforested with the aid of public funds and subsidies. The end product would then be similar to that resulting from the formation of the *Forsthuben*.

Forsthuben

In contrast with the *Zuhuben* the formation of *Forsthuben* brought about much greater and more immediate changes in the landscape. In most cases the buildings fell into ruin very quickly. Afforestation often affected the whole of the former holding, and the site of the old farmsteads can be found only on old maps.

In a few instances new smallholdings for woodcutters were formed with the object of retaining a local source of labour. It has not proved an entirely satisfactory solution, and these *Forsthuben* are experiencing difficulties at the present time. Forest roads are being built or improved, and the woodmen possess motor-bikes or cars which permit them to live in the valley. The arable land going with the houses is of little value because machinery for cultivating it is lacking, and the overtime in forestry or road-making is more lucrative anyway. Furthermore, wives are no longer ready to bear the lonely and hard way of life in the high mountains, which also involves long journeys to school for their children.

Many *Forsthuben* are thus being deserted, and the woodmen settle in the villages in the valleys. The old dual basis of the mountain dweller's life, comparable to some extent to that of a Scottish crofter, will no longer exist in the future. The forest-labourer, earning wages like a townsman and retaining only the right to collect fuel and timber to build a house, will replace him.

The situation is different in those parts of the Alps where scattered settlements have been subject to division amongst heirs. Here the *Walser* settlements of Vorarlberg (Austria) can serve as a model. This high Alpine region at the north-western corner of the Eastern Alps was settled as late as the sixteenth century. There the *Hochtannberg* district affords a classic example of former Alpine pastures, once settled permanently but later becoming an area characterized by various kinds of temporary home.

Today a characteristic mixture of *Winterheimaten* (houses inhabited in winter only), *Vorsässen* (houses at intermediary levels which are occupied in spring and autumn only), and *Almen* (summer ranches) can be observed, all of very similar physical appearance. There is no arable land anywhere in the region; not even potatoes are grown. In the past a special feature of this area, concentrating on stock raising and forage crops, has been for all the members of the family to move from the *Heimgüter*, their low-lying permanent home, to the summer settlements. The abandonment of farmsteads has been encouraged by the fact that they became situated above the timber-line in the course of the centuries because of the misuse of forests. Recently tourist traffic has brought about a re-evaluation of this high mountain region, and depopulation has stopped.

We turn next to nucleated villages with highly fragmented field patterns; western Tyrol (Austria) can serve as an example. This area had been part of the see of Chur (Switzerland) and according to the *Lex Romana Churiensis* there was no limit to the sub-division of lots and even of buildings. Most of the houses, built of stone, are fairly large. They were divided amongst a number of owners in a highly complicated way over the course of the centuries. In the nineteenth century the civil servants of the cadastral office had great difficulties in making an exact survey and in allotting the various parts of the houses to their respective owners. In some cases such houses were the property of as many as six to eight families. It followed that the same number of sheds, dung-heaps, ovens for baking bread, etc., were attached to them. Such division is no longer of importance, since the number of holdings has been diminishing over the past 50 years, but there

Hamlet with fields equally divided among the heirs in the Paznaun, Tyrol (Austria)

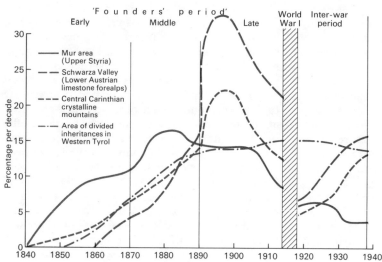

Fig. 6. Stages and extent of the abandonment of settlements

are still houses with two or three owners. As the number of enterprises continues to decrease in this area of small or tiny holdings there will soon, no doubt, be only one family to each house here, too. Generally speaking, this area constitutes the northernmost outpost of a Mediterranean type of agriculture. The arable land is terraced, and there was once a complex system of irrigation. The use of the meadows used to be as highly intensive as that of the arable land (rye, barley, and potatoes higher up; in lower regions maize, too), but it is now losing importance rapidly.

In this region of the Austrian Alps tourist traffic provides an extra income, and commuters are able to find jobs in the industrialized valley. Thus population decline has been halted, the existing buildings are taken care of, and new ones are added. They can be seen on the outskirts of many of the old compact villages.

Similar opportunities did not exist in the Italian Alps. There the rural exodus was furthered by the enormous expansion of industry in the forelands after World War II, mainly along the Milan–Venice motorway. The decay of the settlements high in the mountains and the abandonment of the cultivated land is therefore much more complete in this area of the Southern Alps (Julian Alps, Venetian Alps, Bergamasc Alps), characterized as they are by unfavourable environmental conditions. Furthermore, change is much more evident to the eye as no stands of trees, but only coppices of maquis type, replace the crops.

The extent of change

An example taken from the Austrian Alps will serve to illustrate the different phases of abandonment (Fig. 6). Along the main axis of industrialization of Inner Austria, the Mur and Mürz valleys

in Styria, the height of depopulation was observed as early as the 'Founders' Period' (around 1870), whereas the crisis did not reach its peak until two decades later in the northern limestone ranges of Upper and Lower Austria and in the crystalline mountains of Carinthia further away from industry and traffic routes. A second climax during the inter-war period coincided with the world-wide economic crisis during which many of the mountain farms were sold by auction. At present there is a continuous process of change of the kind described above.

Data concerning the extent of abandonment are limited to the Austrian Alps. In the eastern forest mountains of Styria, Carinthia, and Lower Austria one-half of the farmsteads have disappeared. There are whole valleys and slopes which are no longer populated. Compared with the east the extent of regression in the west is surprisingly small: only 9 per cent of the holdings have ceased to operate over the past 100 years in Northern Tyrol and 15 per cent in Eastern Tyrol. Small enterprises have typically been amalga-

Farmhouse equally divided among four proprietors in a village in the Engadin (Switzerland)

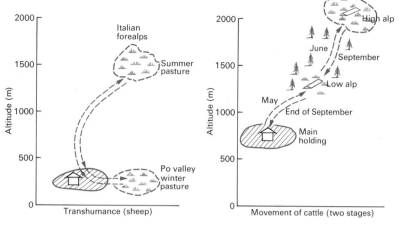

Fig. 7. Types of pastoral economy in the Eastern Alps

mated with larger ones to create more viable units. It should be noted, however, that the abandonment of 'frontier' settlements in the higher parts of the Eastern Alps has much more serious consequences than a similar movement in the lower forested mountains.

The effect on the Alpine economy

The decline of the upper limit of permanent settlement in various parts of the Eastern Alps necessarily induced changes in the zone of seasonal settlement above. This region of Alpine pastures and summer ranches is one of the most important elements in the overall settlement system and economy. Like their permanent counterparts, the seasonal settlements exhibit many variations. To be able to understand their present problems, their characteristic features must first be described (Fig. 7).

There is a fundamental difference between the Italian Alps and the Austrian and German Alps. Only in the former are there old-established forms of transhumance, a type of economy characteristic of the Mediterranean world. It clearly differs from the Alpine stock-breeding economy since it involves the long-distance migration of, principally, sheep. The flocks, looked after by herders, spend the winters on the plains of the Po valley and the summers in the Alps. Normally the pastures are leased for short periods only. Formerly there were fixed routes for the seasonal migration; now lorries are being used to cover the long distances involved.

Of late many of the pastures utilized in winter have been lost due to the land improvements taking place in parts of the Po valley. In consequence transhumance has lost some of its importance. Furthermore, it is increasingly diffi-

cult to find suitable people ready to bear the hardships of a shepherd's life.

In addition to this type of transhumance, there is a seasonal migration of cattle from the Po valley to the neighbouring high Alpine ranges (Bergamasc Alps, Venetian prealps, especially Sette Communi). It is losing ground, also, but it never had any great significance.

With regard to the Alpine pastures, three levels are distinguished and allotted different names: *Nieder-* (low), *Mittel-* (intermediate), and *Hoch-* (high) *alm* (pasture). In the high Alps there is often a complicated system of utilizing these three stages alternately in order to permit a longer grazing season. The Carnic Alps present a good example of this. As it is a system of grazing which involves pastures at different heights and requires more labour, however, it is being abandoned in favour of one which makes use of pastures situated on one level only.

Altitude and accessibility influence the type of economy. Dairy cattle are to be found on the lowest levels only, since the pasture must be rich and there must be easy access for the transport of milk. Young cattle are grazed higher up. Sheep only are herded above the tree-line. The seasonal migration of herds according to the temperature régime is represented in Fig. 8 in an example from Eastern Tyrol.

The systems of ownership differ widely in the various countries and portions of the Alps. There are individual alps★ belonging to a single owner, normally a peasant. Only in Italy and Switzerland is the leasing of alps of some importance. Alps

---

★ The word 'alp' (with a lower case 'a') is used in the sense of a high mountain pasture above the tree-line combined with periodic settlement.

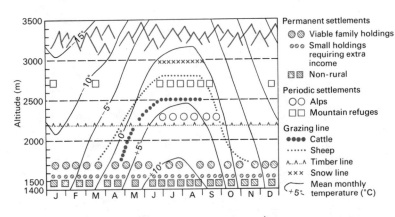

Fig. 8. The relation between temperature and grazing on the alps of the Eastern Tyrol

Permanent settlements
- ⊘⊘ Viable family holdings
- ⊙⊙⊙ Small holdings requiring extra income
- ▨▨ Non-rural

Periodic settlements
- ○○ Alps
- ☐☐ Mountain refuges

Grazing line
- ●●● Cattle
- ⋯⋯ Sheep
- ʌ.ʌ.ʌ Timber line
- ××× Snow line
- ⌒ Mean monthly temperature (°C)

owned by two or more peasants are 'communal', whereas 'servitude alps' belong to the owners of large forest estates (the State, the Church, or private owners). On the latter alps, a certain number of peasants have specific rights to graze their cattle. 'Co-operative alps' are the property of co-operatives specializing in cattle raising.

The structure of land tenure referred to above is highly relevant to the process of abandonment or simply of neglect. Forestry and grazing were difficult to reconcile in the 'servitude alps' for example, because the owners of the large forests had to compensate peasants for the loss of old grazing rights. An F.A.O. enquiry of 1959 collected data on these servitudes (grazing rights). They are represented in Table 2.

The number of individually owned alps increased when *Zuhuben* (second farms) were formed, as described above. On the other hand, individually owned alps higher up fell into disuse. They were most strongly affected by the shortage of labour. The alps owned by co-operatives are normally the ones most subject to improvements. Their position is therefore the least precarious, but their number is fairly small.

In most of the Alpine States statistical data are compiled for the alps (i.e. the pastures), and it is comparatively easy to get information about them. It is much less easy to collect data on the holdings of the peasants in the Alps since no standard definition of this group has been agreed upon so far.

In the Austrian Alps there were 10 819 alps in 1960; 31 per cent of them were 'low' ones, 42 per cent were 'intermediate' alps, and 27 per cent were 'high' ones. About two-thirds were owned by peasants, 25 per cent represented servitudes, and 11 per cent were public property. On average the herds remained on the alps for 100 days. The total was about 700 000 animals, including 110 000 dairy cows, 263 000 young cattle and oxen, 234 000 sheep, and 14 000 horses. Table 3 shows percentages of the different farm animals being grazed on alps in individual Austrian provinces. It reflects the contrast noted above between *Almbauern* in the west and *Waldbauern* in the east.

The value of the alps for Austrian agriculture is not to be underrated. They provide fodder equivalent to the needs of approximately 100 000 head of cattle. As to the kind of animals grazed on the alps, the great number of sheep in the western provinces (Vorarlberg, Tyrol, and Salzburg) is worthy of note. It results from the traditional movement of sheep to the Austrian alps from southern Alpine valleys both in Italy and in Switzerland. The predominant form of utilization is the 'mixed' alp, grazed by dairy cows and young cattle (55 per cent). Alps for dairy cows alone are of importance in Salzburg because of the large cheese factories in the Alpine foreland.

The decrease in the total utilized area of the

TABLE 2

Forest-grazing and litter-gathering rights in the Alps

	Percentage of area affected	
	Grazing rights	Litter gathering rights
Bavaria	35·0	2·3
Austria	26·0	12·5
Italy	29·0	23·4
Switzerland	12·0	7·5

TABLE 3

Percentage of farm animals grazed on alps in Austria

Provinces	dairy cows	young cattle	horses	sheep
Vorarlberg	48·0	71·2	20·4	115·1
Tyrol	43·2	76·3	25·6	151·1
Salzburg	31·8	60·3	32·9	121·4
Carinthia	13·6	46·9	14·3	85·7
Styria	6·8	28·1	8·0	49·3
Upper Austria	0·6	2·3	0·3	3·2
Lower Austria	0·1	2·6	0·1	—
Austria	9·4	22·3	5·4	76·2

TABLE 4
Types of alp and use of labour in Austria (1960)

| | Number of alps utilized for | | | | | Labourers | | |
	dairy cows only	young cattle only	mixed stock	horses	sheep	female	male	total
Vorarlberg	177	124	465	2	5	2 077	201	2 278
Tyrol	171	498	1 562	4	71	5 341	1 009	6 350
Salzburg	346	475	1 461	3	41	2 202	1 483	3 685
Carinthia	85	1 342	695	9	47	1 232	1 184	2 416
Styria	54	1 129	1 472	1	23	1 616	1 479	3 095
Upper Austria	3	59	341			57	364	421
Lower Austria	2	119	23			154	12	166
Total	838	3 746	6019	19	187	12 679	5 732	18 411
Percentage	7·7	34·6	55·7	0·2	1·7	68·9	31·1	100

alps was estimated to be approximately 20 per cent over the period 1961–71. Many of those with unfavourable environmental conditions and with difficult access were abandoned. The decline was particularly marked on those alps concerned only with cattle. A similar trend is to be observed in Switzerland. Whereas there were still 141 000 cows on the Swiss alps in 1955, their number was down to 100 000 in 1965. In contrast with the Austrian Alps, however, there was an increase in the number of young cattle from the forelands summering on the alps. In the German Alps the extent to which the alps were abandoned amounted to about 20 per cent over the period 1954 to 1968. Half of the abandoned alps were afforested.

The number of cattle summered in the Italian Alps fell by approximately 30 per cent during the 1960s. This is due mainly to a reduction in the movement of herds from the Po valley where a dairy industry and stock raising have been introduced. Cattle (Frisian breeds) are being grazed here on enclosed pastures in summer as well as winter. It is easy to appreciate why, in both

High alpine pasture (*Luggner-alm*) against the Grossglockner (3798 m): Carinthia (Austria)

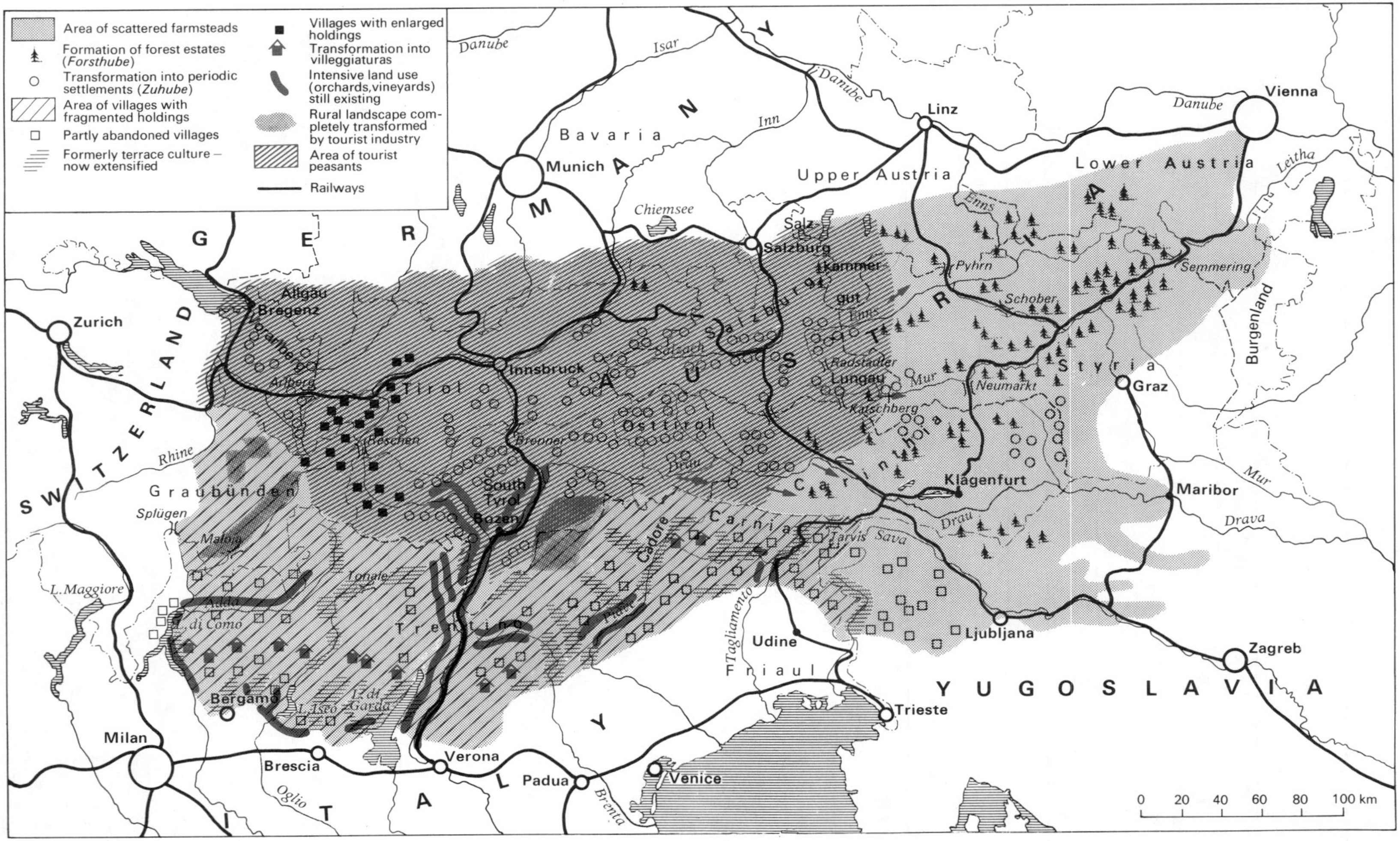

Map 2. Types of mountain peasantry in the Eastern Alps

Legend:

Area of scattered farmsteads

Formation of forest estates (*Forsthube*)

Transformation into periodic settlements (*Zuhube*)

Area of villages with fragmented holdings

Partly abandoned villages

Formerly terrace culture – now extensified

Villages with enlarged holdings

Transformation into villeggiaturas

Intensive land use (orchards, vineyards) still existing

Rural landscape completely transformed by tourist industry

Area of tourist peasants

Railways

Place names and features:

Vienna, Linz, Munich, Zurich, Milan, Venice, Padua, Verona, Brescia, Bergamo, Trieste, Ljubljana, Zagreb, Maribor, Graz, Klagenfurt, Salzburg, Innsbruck, Udine, Bregenz

Countries/regions: GERMANY, SWITZERLAND, ITALY, YUGOSLAVIA, Bavaria, Bayern, Lower Austria, Upper Austria, Burgenland, Styria, Carinthia, Tirol, South Tirol, Ostirol, Trentino, Friaul, Cadore, Graubünden, Allgäu

Rivers/lakes: Danube, Inn, Isar, Chiemsee, Salz, Ems, Mur, Drava, Drau, Save, Sava, Gail, Tagliamento, Brenta, Oglio, Rhine, L. Maggiore, L. di Como, L. di Garda, Adige, Splügen

Other: Semmering, Schober, Pyhrn, Neumarkt, Katschberg, Hammerau, Lungau, Radstadt

Austria and Switzerland, the only cattle now being bred are ones that adapt easily to the pastures in low-lying areas as well as alps.

The deserted alps in Italy have not been afforested systematically as they have in Austria. Furthermore, the seeds carried by the wind do not grow into trees either, on account of the dry summers. Most of the former alps have therefore become wilderness areas. The province of Carnia is the only one to date where afforestation has attained some importance. The Italian Alps exhibit the most outmoded elements of a mountain pastoral economy, evidenced not only in the appearance of the buildings but also in the methods of dairy production. It is clearly a result of the fact that the rural exodus was very marked in this area of fragmented holdings. The remaining population is in consequence composed mainly of higher age groups, showing little initiative for introducing innovations.

Recently Italian government policies with regard to agriculture have become less equivocal. Although there is help of a local kind for the Alps, interest and public funds concentrate heavily upon other areas such as the Po valley and southern Italy. The Italian Alps thus remain a marginal area.

The rise of forestry and hunting

During the past century the relative importance of forestry and agriculture in the Alps has undergone a marked change. For many centuries the exploitation of the woodlands had been ancillary to the agricultural enterprises. Little attention had been paid to the forests, and thus timber was of limited value and it tended to be utilized wastefully as fuel or in building fences and houses. Cattle were grazed in the woods, litter was collected, and twigs were cut from deciduous trees in order to provide extra fodder. Amongst these extensive types of land-use there was a kind of shifting cultivation, limited mainly to Styria and carried on as late as the 1930s. The areas formerly used in this way can still be identified by the groups of alders and birch trees amongst the spruce forests. When the stands were 20 to 25 years old, the trees were felled and the undergrowth was fired. The soil was then cultivated by the use of a hoe. Rye was sown in the first year, oats in the second. Because of the sprouting of alders, the area could not normally be used for crops after the second year.

In an attempt to enlarge the total area of alps, the upper limit of tree-growth was gradually lowered in the western high valleys of the Tyrol and of Vorarlberg, even as late as the start of the present century. Not only this, but breaches were made in protective forest tracts so that avalanches were able to find their way right down into the valleys. Paradoxically, the lack of fuel and difficulties of obtaining timber very often caused the closing down of alps later on.

On the whole, an efficient forestry was not carried on by the peasants until fairly recently. Generally speaking, it did not start until the later nineteenth century, when the example set by large forest estates began to be followed. The latter had initiated well-planned forestry as early as the period of mercantilism, during the eighteenth century, though at first it was confined to the northern parts of the Eastern Alps.

The nature of land ownership differs widely between the various States of the Alps, which is one of the reasons why forests have varying economic importance for the mountain peasants. After extensive clearances had taken place in the Eastern Alps during the Middle Ages, large areas remained the property of the Crown or the Church, as well as of seigneurs. This was true mainly in the northern limestone ranges. Thus 71 per cent of the Bavarian forests are public property; whereas in Austria the State does not possess, on average, more than 15 per cent, and individual peasants own 54 per cent. In Switzerland, on the other hand, forests owned by communes or corporations predominate (84 per cent). The fairly low proportion of 57 per cent of the forests with common ownership in Italy is caused by the special situation of the province of Bozen (Trentino-Tiroler Etschland) where forests owned individually by peasants prevail.

The differences of ownership also result in varying standards of upkeep. Public forests and large private estates clearly occupy first rank. Those owned by peasants represent an intermediate stage, whereas the communal forests have been exploited wastefully and now consist only of coppices and scrub in the Southern Alps. This degradation does not follow entirely from the nature of ownership, however, but is also due to the grazing of goats and sheep. The nature of forest operations is relevant, too. The natural vegetation consists of deciduous trees almost up to the timber-line, of oaks in the lower parts, and of beeches higher up; and the management of coppices has predominated for a long time. Large areas are covered by the coppiced bushes of deciduous species (alders, oaks, hornbeam, willows, sweet chestnut, robinias), but the Mediterranean climatic conditions—sudden downpours and summer droughts—very often bring about the complete devastation of the coppices.

The grassland district of Hochtannberg, Vorarlberg (Austria) offers a characteristic mixture of permanent settlement and alps.

The areas of limestone and sandstone are especially vulnerable to soil erosion. Extremely high investment is necessary to ensure the success of afforestation here, since it is very difficult to bring back forest, even pinewoods, to completely barren slopes robbed of their soil.

To what extent do forests provide an income for the mountain peasants? The proportion is 15 per cent on average in the Austrian Alps, but it rises to 30 per cent or more in the east, where forests occupy an area several times larger than that of the arable land. In the west forestry is hampered by the fact that 23 per cent of all Austrian forests have to serve as protective woodland, in which the felling of trees is limited by strict regulations. Austria, however, is exceptional, and elsewhere the importance of the forest to the mountain peasants is much less: in Switzerland only 2 per cent of their income is derived from forestry.

Where profit is concerned, the argument is always in favour of forestry. Depending on the size of the enterprise, it yields three to four times higher wages per hour than does agriculture. Compared with the production of fodder and the rearing of cattle, forestry clearly has many advantages on steeper slopes where tractors cannot be used, as well as on shady slopes which provide excellent conditions for growing trees. It is little wonder that there is a general tendency amongst many peasants in the German and Austrian Alps as well as in Southern Tyrol (Italy) to afforest pastures and even arable land at increasing distances from the homesteads.

As noted above there is a group of large private forest estates, the owners of which are anxious to add to their property. They always aim first at enlarging and rounding off their estates in order to minimize the high cost of infra-structure (forest roads, etc.) and of careful preparation of the land. Here is another reason for the extension of the total forest area, especially in the Austrian Alps.

One of the most interesting features of the post-war period, especially in the large forests, has been a marked increase in the number of game. It is related to the growing importance of hunting as an exclusive sport of the well-to-do. A census carried out in the Bavarian Alps in 1968 showed that the number of deer had increased by five to ten times. There is more game than cattle in this area now.

This phenomenon has caused problems for forestry. Although grazing rights in the woods have been abolished and thus damage brought about by grazing cattle (trampling down of seedlings, biting off of shoots, etc.) is kept down, the excess of game constitutes an even graver danger to the mountain forests. The contraction in the number of high Alpine pastures influences the location of game. Forest experts observe that game 'follows' the cattle. When only the lower alps are stocked with cattle, the surrounding forests are invaded by game who cause a great deal of damage by stripping the bark from the trees.

This fact has been realized by the majority of sportsmen, but no counter-measures have been taken so far. The reason for this situation is to be found in the complicated system of the leasing of hunting rights to social groups little interested in forestry. The income to be derived from the leasing of hunting rights can be estimated from the premium paid for shooting a roebuck, namely 15 000 to 30 000 Austrian shillings. This is nearly as much as an Austrian mountain peasant can obtain when selling a two-year-old fattened ox or bull.

2 Readjustment of the Mountain Peasantry

Self-aid measures

The self-aid measures of the peasants fall into two categories: rationalization within the enterprise, and co-operation between enterprises.

Traditional mountain farming was characterized by diversified land-use on small or minute plots, aiming at self-sufficiency and making use of a great deal of labour. To this system we owe the fact that grain cultivation was pushed to the absolute limits set by physical conditions in the Alps. Small fields of rye and potatoes are still remembered as having existed around the highest permanent settlements in the Eastern Alps, the Rofenhöfe in the Ötz valley (western Austria, 2009 m) in 1900. Until quite recently grain was grown by most of the mountain peasants. Only during the past 10 years has a really marked change set in, most notably in the western parts of the Austrian Alps. Most of the former arable land has now been transformed into permanent grassland. The livestock economy is still a mixed one but the fattening of two or four oxen a year has been replaced by dairy farming and the fattening of calves. Small flocks of sheep, once important, are no longer to be found in many areas. Pigs and poultry are of some significance but for the local market only. Horse breeding has been given up.

Progress in mechanization and in the construction of new farm buildings can be considered a good clue to progress in adapting to the new conditions. Over the past two decades, intensive building activity has led to the replacement of ancient farmsteads in the greater part of the Eastern Alps. This trend began in the valley settlements and subsequently spread to the higher regions. Wooden structures were most affected: many traditional types of homestead, such as the clustered homesteads of Carinthia were quick to disappear. To save something of this cultural heritage, old rural buildings were acquired hastily in the Austrian provinces of Carinthia and Styria and re-erected in open-air museums. The unit-house typical of Salzburg, the Tyrol, and Bavaria held its own, however, and was modernized, thanks to strict building regulations.

In connection with the rebuilding movement it is worth stressing that although the peasants have been able to augment their earnings during phases of general economic prosperity, mechanization and the renovation of buildings have, in most cases, been possible only because they were content to accept a lower-than-average standard of living. Even though their produce may have found a ready market there was insufficient cash both to improve the house and to stock it with consumer goods.

The question arises: will the next generation of mountain peasants be ready to make a similar sacrifice, necessary to compensate for the disparity in income between town and country? In the past the traditional attitude of the rural population to the acquisition of property has prevented them 'solving' the problem by simply abandoning their way of life, but attitudes are changing as more is learned of town ways.

The co-operative movement has antecedents in some parts of the Alps, especially in the south. There the *Waale*—ditches channelling the water from mountain torrents for the irrigation of meadows, fields, orchards, and vineyards and perhaps extending several kilometres—are still admired by travellers. Collective ownership of certain forests and pastures had a sociological and psychological importance for the population, helping to offset the loneliness of the high mountains, besides having economic advantages. The wealth of customs and usages, all related to the annual cycle of rural activities and communal life, has become a vast field of study for Alpine folklorists. Co-operation amongst neighbours was not confined to the villages, but occurred in the scattered settlements also, whenever it was necessary to cope with particularily laborious tasks, such as weeding the growing crops in spring, harvesting the grain, or threshing. Naturally, much of this neighbourly help disappeared when crop farming was abandoned and the amount of labour available decreased.

More recently co-operation amongst mountain peasants has successfully extended to the building of access roads and cableways. In addition there are various types of buildings intended for communal use, such as cold-storage depots, smoking huts and ovens in Styria, potato cellars in the Lungau (Salzburg), and facilities for drying fodder in the Styrian Mur and Enns valleys, in the Allgäu, and in Switzerland.

Under the sponsorship of the *Schweizerische Arbeitsgemeinschaft der Bergbauern* organization

(SAB), schemes for self-help were started among the peasants for the construction or renovation of houses, stables, and other farm buildings (silos, manure pits, machine-sheds, wells, etc.) as well as for the construction of approach roads. For this purpose rural co-operatives were founded and managed on the cost-price principle. They are able to acquire the materials needed at much lower prices than can the individual farmer. Sometimes they are active only during those periods of the year in which there is little work on the farms. In this way the mountain peasants can contribute labour and do part of the work themselves. In order that their activities may be organized effectively, the applications of the members are collected and integrated into a general plan that is scrutinized by the official authorities granting the funds.

Opinions differ as to the value of machinery co-operatives, which on the whole have not been very successful. Much more efficient are machine rings, made up of a number of peasants who generally use their own machines on their own land but also make them available for use by other members. Though such rings might be very useful in the mountains because of the different dates of harvests in lower and higher regions, they are more or less limited to those areas where tractors are serviceable.

Co-operative management is of great importance to forestry, also. Peasants have formed

A 'forest peasant' taking his timber to the valley in winter

associations to build roads in forests that had not hitherto been accessible and to organize the marketing of their timber. There are a number of examples of the co-operative afforestation of former pastures (Carinthia).

In the Southern Alps (Southern Tyrol, Trentino, and Friaul) co-operative byres have been built. The joint proprietors, normally owning two or three cows each, are under no obligation to provide labour, but they have to supply a certain amount of fodder, according to the number of shares they hold.

Associations for the fattening and marketing of cattle, encountered both in the valleys and in higher regions, represent a new type of co-operative. A ring founded in southern Carinthia in 1968 affords an excellent example. Based on the reports of individual members, the manager makes arrangements with regard to the number of cattle to be sold and the date when they will be delivered to export firms or beef processing plants. The stables for fattening cattle are controlled by the Chambers of Agriculture. If this trend continues, rural associations in the future will not limit their activities to production, but will organize the marketing also.

Extra sources of income

Reference has already been made to the mountain peasants' traditional dependence on extra sources of income. In only a very few cases has it been possible to establish new sources of income which are in any way comparable with the old ones, such as carting and carrying, floating and transporting timber, and producing such wooden articles as shingles, sleepers, and supports for vines. Where a solution has been sought it has usually been in the form of cottage industries. In Bavaria hats, gloves, nails, woodcarvings, and woven goods are manufactured. The Gröden valley in Southern Tyrol has succeeded in gaining a world-wide market for its woodcarvings. A technical school has been founded and the putting-out system organized with the help of urban capital. These attempts have, however, been successful only locally, and most of the mountain peasants have been forced to seek extra income elsewhere. Daily commuting forms part of their existence. Mountain peasants work as woodcutters and in sawmills, with firms constructing roads or power plants, and in the field of avalanche- and flood-control. Fortunately official authorities will often insist on the use of local peasant labour when placing orders with private firms.

In view of this situation it is hardly surprising that the members of parliament representing

TABLE 5
Income derived from agriculture and forestry (AF) and extra income (E) in Austrian
Buchführungsbetriebe *(Austrian schillings per worker)*

	Crop farms in the Alpine foreland			Grassland farms in the high Alps		
Year	AF	E	Total	AF	E	Total
1960	8 690	2 337	11 027	8 210	4 450	12 660
1962	8 489	3 809	12 298	7 122	6 404	13 526
1964	11 541	4 787	16 323	8 949	9 230	18 179
1966	12 960	6 114	19 074	10 653	11 241	21 849
1968	19 174	6 057	25 231	7 342	15 787	23 129

rural constituencies should strongly advocate that industry be directed to the mountains as a means of providing jobs for the surplus labour of the small farms and of checking the rural exodus. Such a policy raises the whole question of integrating mountain communities into a large-scale regional plan, an idea that will be explored below. Meanwhile, politicians still have to face up to the shorter-term problems arising from peasant enterprises that are not viable without additional income. Many of them believe that there is no room for the Alpine peasants in the modern industrialized world. If such a view becomes general, the chances are bleak of rural holdings surviving in extensive areas of the Alps. In this connection it is illuminating to contrast the yields of Austrian *Buchführungsbetriebe* (efficient farms in the Alpine foreland, run in a modern way and giving yields above average), with those in the high Alps (Table 5). Note the dependence in the high Alps on 'extra income'. Here is proof of the great importance attached to the provision of jobs in the Alpine regions and to the intensification of tourist traffic as a means of securing the very survival of the mountain peasantry.

Public aid

Up to about 1970 it was stressed repeatedly that all public measures for supporting mountain peasants were to be considered a kind of stopgap welfare policy that could not be sustained indefinitely. Furthermore, the mechanization and rationalization of farms in the lowlands was causing the differences in income derived from agriculture and forestry in the lowlands and in the Alpine regions to increase steadily. The spokesmen for trade and commerce argued that there should be no subsidies for agriculture in the high mountains where production had been proved to be more expensive than elsewhere. The peasants of the lowlands pointed out that there was almost sufficient food produced for the domestic market

without the contribution of the mountains, that there was in any case a surplus of dairy products and even, as in Austria, of cattle that had to be exported, and that there was thus no need for agricultural production in the Alpine regions.

This was, to all intents and purposes, the view expressed and defended by the vice-president of the E.E.C., Sicco L. Mansholt, at the F.A.O. conference in Rome in September 1962. He claimed that the mountainous areas should be afforested since the peasants living there were unable to compete with those of the lowlands. In his statement, repeated later in slightly modified versions, he failed to appreciate the new role taken on by the areas traditionally occupied by the mountain peasantry in the Alps, namely that of a recreation area for Europe's industrial society. In order to cater fully for this new role, it is absolutely vital to preserve the cultural landscape in the high mountains. The problem of the mountain peasantry has thus been transferred from the field of economic politics to that of social politics.

Recently this change of emphasis has become obvious within the E.E.C. also. On 22 February 1973 the Dutch European Commissioner Pierre Lardionis announced in Brussels a ten-year plan for an extensive scheme of subsidies for the mountain peasants of the E.E.C. Although the total amount is not a very large one, the very fact that such a scheme has been put forward at all demonstrates a fundamental change in the assessment of the mountain peasants' role in present-day society. Several of the possibilities and limitations of public measures are outlined below.

Price policy measures

The old division of functions between the mountains and the lowlands has undergone significant change since the inter-war period. Cattle raising, formerly limited to the Alpine regions, has been introduced to the Upper Austrian and Bavarian Alpine foreland and has, in part, yielded better results there. The former, in particular, has become an export-oriented region for cattle breeding. Mechanization and certain changes in the pattern of meat consumption have brought about a reduced demand for oxen. Raising them had been the traditional activity of many mountain peasants who thus lost their distinctive role with regard to stock breeding. However, they gained the new function of supplying milk to the urban market. The price of milk in the realm of mountain peasant policy has, therefore, come to occupy a similar position to wages in industrial politics. Manipulation of the controlled milk price always has serious consequences in the high mountain areas.

In 1968 an attempt was made to reduce the supply of milk and to get rid of a surplus of butter by means of lowering the milk price. The effect was the opposite of that desired, since the mountain peasants did their best to produce even more milk in order to make up for their loss of income. Utilization of grassland was intensified, forests and pastures were demarcated more exactly, the construction of roads was accelerated, and stricter rules were announced for quality controls of the milk and for selective breeding. Once more it had become obvious that the mountain peasants base their budgets on earned income and do not consider longer-term interests on capital invested. Yet in spite of all this, the supply of milk did in fact diminish overall since many of the large farms in the forelands gave up dairying altogether or to some extent and concentrated instead on crop farming. Finally it is worth noting that the price of milk is unlikely ever to reach in the future a level high enough to cover actual costs of production in the high mountains. In Austria and in Southern Tyrol the milk produced is subsidized by levelling the transport costs to attain a uniform production price at all locations.

Subsidies and credit

Direct and indirect grants as well as credits for investment are given to the mountain peasants in order to make up for the disparity of incomes between the Alpine regions and the forelands. Such a policy requires a legally fixed boundary to the areas of mountain peasantry. In Bavaria such a boundary was laid down in 1955, embracing 156 communes with 14 200 enterprises. The Italian Mountain Act of 1952 demarcated the area of rehabilitation where public funds are to be invested for improving the agricultural structures.

Between 1944 and 1947 areas of mountain peasantry were delimited in Switzerland. They include 67 500 enterprises as compared with the 95 000 enterprises in valley areas. Similar criteria were applied in Austria. Some 1626, or 40 per cent of her 4039 communes, were classified as mountain communes. They have 123 000 farm holdings, the largest number of any European country. In 1961 a special register of mountain holdings was drawn up in Austria which identifies the climatic conditions and the location of all the lots as well as details of their accessibility.

Public aid includes both direct supplementation of income—family incomes below a certain level have been complemented in Switzerland since 1954—and indirect grants. These latter measures are of greatest importance in Switzerland where there are premiums for stock farming, for fodder grains, and for bread grains as well as premiums for flour based on home-grown grain. Furthermore, there are grants for the cultivation of potatoes at heights above 1000 m.

Further measures are designed to assist livestock production. The attempts at improving the marketing of cattle and pigs are particularly impressive. The breeding of quality animals is encouraged by premiums, but there are premiums also for the elimination of substandard livestock. Contributions are also made to assist sales, markets, etc., as well as for transport. Concentrated feed and hay are supplied cheaply in those mountainous areas where unfavourable weather conditions bring about a shortage of fodder.

Socio-political measures aim at a general improvement of living conditions in the Alpine regions. In 1971 a standard pension for peasants was introduced in Austria, and thus a new form of provision for old age was created. This, in turn, encourages the transferring of a farm from an old man to his son at an earlier date than would otherwise have been the case. The construction of approach roads and the introduction of school-bus services have, in part, removed an educational problem. The cost of boarding schools is paid in order to give children of peasant families a chance to go to secondary school.

All these trends demonstrate that agrarian policy in the Alpine region is still concerned with the family holding. But the emphasis in all countries has shifted from direct aid towards an improvement of the infrastructure. The construction of approach roads to homesteads and alps has therefore been promoted as well as tracks for the transport of timber and cableways for carrying goods. In Austria 70 000 km of track have been made passable for tractors and cars. Other projects supported by credits include the restoration of buildings, the supply of water

Rural settlement in the Cadore (Italian Alps). Whereas the settlement is developing rapidly because of tourist traffic, the fragmented, formerly intensively cultivated arable land is no longer used

and electricity, and the construction of manure pits, silos, and drier installations. Afforestation enters into the programmes, as do avalanche-control and irrigation projects. The mechanization of mountain holdings is everywhere promoted by cheap credit, and the consolidation of farmland and measures in communal forests and on alps are also involved.

Basic policy documents have recently been drawn up in all the Alpine countries. In 1969 both the Bavarian Alpine Plan and the Italian Mountain Act were passed. Austria's programme for the mountainous areas and the Swiss equivalent followed in 1970. These plans have resulted in a complete re-evaluation of the role of the mountain peasantry. The main objective is no longer considered production, but rather conservation and the provision of social services for modern society. In this context the Hessian Minister for Food, Agriculture, and Forests suggested as long ago as 1965 that a way to remunerate the peasants for their contribution to conservation was with a flat sum of 100 DM per hectare. At that time he was dismissed as a 'romanticist', although similar views are now commonly being expressed.

In 1970 a system of grants was adopted for the preservation of grassland in Southern Tyrol. The maximum amount payable is 20 000 lira per hectare or 200 000 lira per enterprise. It is regarded as compensation for adverse working conditions on steep slopes and at great heights. In the same year the Bavarian Diet passed an act for the promotion of the rural landscape. Here, for the first time, a German act obliges the State to take care of man-made landscapes. In Liechtenstein each peasant receives 300 francs for each head of cattle he keeps and a maximum of 4500 francs per holding for the summer pasturing of cattle. In this way an attempt is made to prevent alps at high elevations from remaining uncultivated.

The costs of conservation without any contribution from the peasants themselves are very high, as was learned in the Spessart in West Germany. There, as a result of population loss, vast areas are lying fallow, yet they have to be mowed. For this the forest authorities in charge have to spend 200–300 DM per hectare. This kind of conservation, utilizing special working groups, will always be expensive for public authorities.

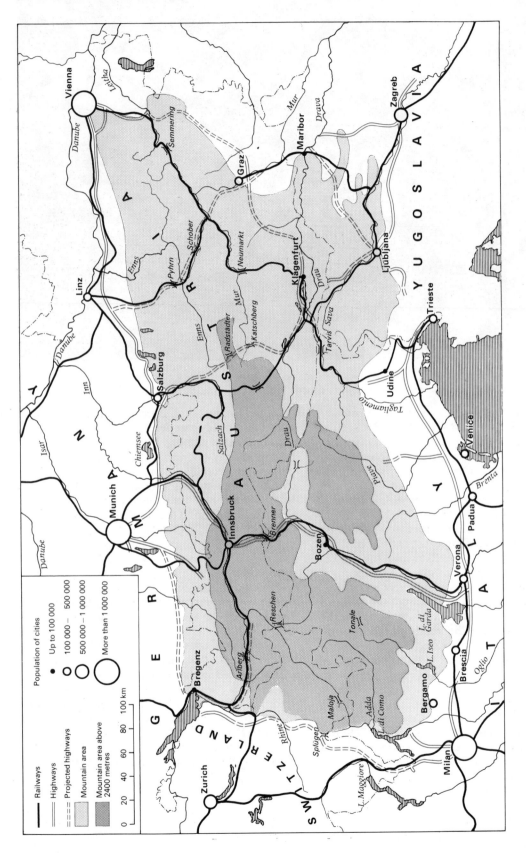

Map 3. Main traffic routes in the Eastern Alps

3 Tourism and Recreation

The Eastern Alps: a region of transit

Separating political powers, economic regions, and cultural areas, the Alps have traditionally constituted a region of passage. North–south routeways corresponding with physiographically defined passages have been used since Roman times. During the Middle Ages, Graubünden and the Tyrol came into existence as routeway States.

The most important pass of the Eastern Alps is the Brenner Pass (1371 m), since it permits the Alps to be crossed with a single ascent at one of their widest points. Its importance for traffic dates back to Roman times and did not diminish during the Middle Ages. Almost half of the military expeditions of the German emperors against Italy passed through it. In 1762 a new road was opened which was used by more than 25 000 vehicles a year before the railway line was constructed. The Brenner's role in relation to European transport is underlined by the fact that it was the first pass to be traversed by a transcontinental highway. In 1970 about 3 million cars and trucks passed through it in both directions. As compared with the Brenner, the passes further west, notably the Reschen (1508 m) and the Graubünden Passes (Maloja 1717 m, Splügen 2117 m), are of limited importance with regard to modern tourism based on cars and buses.

Owing to the widening of the Alps towards the east, through-routes involving a single ascent are not possible there. In addition to the old roads from Salzburg to Carinthia (Katschberg 1641 m, Radstädter Tauern 1730 m), the Grossglockner High Alpine Road was constructed between 1930 and 1935 (length: 25 km; summit: Hochtor 2505 m; more than 2·5 million visitors in 1970). Whereas this road is closed in winter, a new road over the Felber Tauern with a tunnel of 5·2 km length permits safe travel from north to south all the year round.

Reflecting the traditional importance of the Brenner route, a railway line was built in 1864–7, the first one in a north-south direction over the Alps. It provided a link between Bavaria and Italy, whereas the Tauern railway line, constructed in 1905–8 (length of tunnel: 8·5 km), linked Bavaria to the Balkan countries (Belgrade and Trieste). It was not possible, however, to revive traffic over the Graubünden Passes by means of a railway line. There the emphasis shifted to the western Swiss Alps. Now the Gotthard and Simplon Passes share the through-traffic.

In contrast with traffic in a north–south direction, that from east to west and vice versa was always of limited importance. Demand within the mountains themselves was too small to encourage the establishment of connections of more than local significance. Furthermore, the east–west axes of European transport systems have always tended to favour routes outside the Alps, in the Alpine foreland to the north or the Po valley to the south. Hence the wide longitudinal valleys, owing their presence to structural features, could attract traffic over certain sections only. When the Austrian State came into existence in 1918 and had the task of creating an efficient west–east connection, the Arlberg route gained in importance. But even this line makes use only of the Inn and Salzach valleys, and avoids the logical continuation through the Enns valley by turning north to Salzburg and the Alpine foreland. The inter-city express train from Innsbruck

The Europa Bridge on the Brenner motorway south of Innsbruck, seen against the Serle (2719 m)

The track of Europe's oldest mountain railway line, over the Semmering, seen against the Rax (Lower Austria)

to Salzburg does not even follow the Salzach valley but reaches the Bavarian Alpine foreland by way of the Inn valley.

The so-called 'transverse routes' (*Schräger Durchgang*) are of much greater importance than the longitudinal valleys. The one connecting Vienna with Trieste (or Rome) occupies first rank amongst these (Semmering Pass 985 m, between the Vienna Basin and Styria; Neumarkt Saddle 984 m, leading to Carinthia; Saddle of Tarvis 813 m, leading to Italy). The very first Alpine railway line with its still-famous stretch over the Semmering was constructed along this route (1848–54). Having been part of a transverse route from Prague to Agram during the Austro-Hungarian Empire, the connection between Linz and Graz over the Phyrn Pass (945 m) and the Schober Pass (849 m) have lately grown in importance to cater for traffic within Austria itself.

This role of the Eastern Alps as a region of passage is a necessary introduction to the study of tourism, since the network of both roads and railways determines the points of entry used by tourist traffic.

The growth of tourism

The beginnings of Alpine tourism are to be found in the pre-railway era. Three types can be distinguished. The oldest example is associated with the extensive forest estates of the northern limestone Alps where hunting had become at an early date the exclusive pastime of the court and the nobility. The Salzkammergut provides an excellent example of this type. It had been the summer residence of the Austrian emperors up to 1918, and it is particularly interesting since it also provides an example of the second type of tourist resort—the spa. Mineral (brine-baths in Bad Ischl) or thermal springs (sodium springs of Bad Gastein) encouraged the development of spas in several places, and these became increasingly popular during the first half of the nineteenth century. A third type of tourism—mountaineering—also came into existence early in the nineteenth century. In this case the Central Alps (Engadin, Ötz valley, and the Dolomites of the Southern Tyrol) were the most popular areas, attracting many foreign climbers.

When the railways were constructed, tourist traffic started to invade the Alpine areas along them, but as yet there was little development of what may be termed popular tourism. Generally speaking, the travellers, who liked to spend the summer in one of the palatial new Grand Hotels, were still drawn from the upper-middle classes.

Attractively situated towns, such as Meran and Bozen in Southern Tyrol or Kitzbühel in Northern Tyrol, became the main centres of tourist traffic. The Semmering Pass drew not only

30

the upper classes of Vienna but those of Budapest, too. The higher parts of the Engadin in Switzerland (St. Moritz, Davos, and Arosa), the Dolomites in Southern Tyrol, and the Gastein valley had already attained the status of international tourist centres before the outbreak of World War I. Mountaineering had become by that time an activity of increasing importance. The Alpine Club had built about 650 refuges in the Eastern Alps in the years before World War I, 302 of them in the Central Alps, 190 in the southern limestone ranges.

The role played by tourist traffic in the favoured portions of the Eastern Alps before World War I can be appreciated from data for the Tyrol. In 1906 the yearly takings of tourist traffic amounted to 60–70 million crowns, whereas the tax revenue of the country as a whole was only 17 million crowns. In the Alpine countries of the Austro–Hungarian Empire, 2·5 million guests were registered in 1909: 884 000 of them stayed in the Tyrol. Even before World War I a number of transport arteries had been built exclusively for tourist traffic, mainly rack-railways, but also cable-railways, such as one on the Zugspitze which served as the main attraction for Munich guests, and one on the Rax for Vienna tourists. Some of the railway lines gained additional importance through tourist traffic, for example the one to Mariazell, a Styrian place of pilgrimage, famous since the seventeenth century, that had earlier been served by paths leading to it. This shrine had attracted more than 100 groups of pilgrims a year (up to 300 000 persons). Tourism combined with military strategy to encourage the construction of new roads such as the Stilfserjoch road, the Jaufen, and the Dolomites road (Southern Tyrol).

During the inter-war period the nature of tourist traffic did not change fundamentally. It was still mainly the upper and the upper-middle classes that visited the Alps. Within easier travel distance of large cities, however, a new kind of summer holiday resort to accommodate the lower-middle classes was beginning to develop. Statistical data on tourist traffic in Austria for 1924 provides some information on this trend. Almost one-third of the 15 million nights registered were spent by people from Vienna alone, and one-third ·by foreigners. Among the latter, visitors from Eastern Europe made up a large majority and only one-third of them were Germans.

At this time there was already a marked difference between the Western and the Eastern Alps with regard to the country of origin of the visitors, a contrast which has undergone little

change to the present day. Thus the Swiss Alps constituted a tourist area of international character, whereas the western provinces of Austria (Tyrol, Vorarlberg, Salzburg) were visited by tourists mainly from Germany. The summer resorts of the eastern part of Austria, the Carinthian lakes and those of the Salzkammergut were mostly in demand by the holiday-makers of Vienna.

In the Italian Alps a similar contrast between western and eastern parts had begun to develop in the inter-war period. Whereas the proportion of foreigners, mainly Germans, was fairly high in Southern Tyrol, especially in the Dolomites, the forealps bordering the Po valley and the Veltlin were frequented increasingly by the citizens of northern Italian towns, notably Milan.

Trends in tourism

Since World War II the make-up of tourist traffic has undergone fundamental changes. New kinds have appeared whereas older ones, unable to adapt to modern conditions, have declined. This is true, for example, of mountaineering. Nowadays its system of refuges does not provide the level of comfort that the Alpinists expect. Further, the exclusive hotels of the 'Founders' Period' no longer draw the well-to-do visitors able to afford a stay there.

The means of transport have changed, too. In 1954 only 19 per cent of the tourists in Austria used their own cars, in 1966 the proportion was 57 per cent, and it has been estimated that it will have reached 63 per cent by 1975. This shift has caused the railways to lose a great deal of their earlier importance and has extended tourist traffic to areas far away from the rail network into large parts of the Eastern Alps, including districts that had not previously been visited at all.

Increasing urbanization, higher incomes for larger groups of the population, and a shortening of the working hours have been factors causing a big increase in the amount of travel generated by the industrialized countries of Western Europe.

Such an increase in travel makes its effect felt in a number of ways, all to be observed in the Alpine regions.

1. A growing number of people tend to spend their holidays abroad. West Germany is of paramount importance as far as tourist traffic in the Alps is concerned, with 50 per cent of Germans travelling to foreign countries for their holidays.

2. In connection with this latter trend there is a tendency to split up the annual holiday. As a result, winter tourism is gaining in importance

and is obviously of greatest significance at high elevations where there is a second tourist season.

3. In addition there is a tendency towards taking a short holiday whenever a 'long weekend' (with one or two days added) offers an opportunity. This is closely connected with

4. the development of recreation areas within weekend travel time of 'million cities', such as Munich, Vienna, or Milan. A study of the short recreational trips undertaken by Munich citizens (1969) provides the following figures for distances covered:

Distances covered	Percentage of the tourists
up to 30 km	20
30–100 km	40
100–250 km	33
more than 250 km	7

Similar data for Vienna are also available: the average distance covered during a one-day trip amounts to 100–200 km and this rises to 300 km for a trip lasting two days.

5. The trends towards taking short holidays and going on trips lasting just a few days both induce a strong movement to acquire second homes in the hinterlands of large cities.

Within the Eastern Alps there have been significant changes in the past decade with regard to the importance of tourist traffic in various areas. In particular, Austria has been able to overtake Switzerland, formerly much more important for tourism (Table 6). Easy access from West Germany and lower prices in comparison with Switzerland both explain the growing attraction of Austria, especially to foreign tourists, whilst strong local initiative and public subsidies have also helped.

Importance of tourism

Tourism has become a mass phenomenon during the second half of the twentieth century and, as such, is of importance in three ways.

1. It provides recreation for the urban population of the European industrialized countries. Because of the growing ease of travel there will be still greater demands on landscapes suitable for recreation, and the Alpine region constitutes an area offering many natural advantages.

2. Tourism is popular with governments since it provides a valuable source of income for those areas of otherwise limited economic potential. This includes areas where, for example, there are few locational attractions favouring industrialization and limited public funds to provide for it. Though the opportunity of creating new jobs must not be over-estimated in regions with a fairly short season, tourism can give an extra impetus to local economic development, increasing the tax revenue and, in many cases, halting the exodus of population.

3. The contribution of tourism to the national economy varies widely within the Eastern Alps. It is of greatest importance in Austria, where as early as 1961/2 the revenue from tourist traffic amounted to about 12 per cent of the total income. Of this, 80 per cent was derived from foreign tourists, yielding a total of 9 thousand million AS in foreign currency, and covering 98·2 per cent of the deficit in foreign trade. Regional differences are fairly great, however. The Tyrol's share was 7200 AS per inhabitant; Burgenland provided only 188 AS per head.

In 1971 the takings in foreign currency amounted to 31·7 thousand million AS, but

TABLE 6

The development of tourist traffic in Austria and in Switzerland during the 1960s

	1960		1970	
	Austria	Switzerland	Austria	Switzerland
	thousands		thousands	
Beds in hotels, boarding houses, etc.	280	203	522	261
in supplementary lodgings	267	18	470	—
Foreign tourists	4 553	4 949	9 588	6 920
Overnight stays of foreign tourists	25 708	15 977	67 405	21 364
Average length of stay of foreigners (days)	5·6	3·2	7·0	3·1

because of the large sum spent by Austrian tourists abroad the surplus was reduced to 22 thousand million AS. It just sufficed to cover 86 per cent of the foreign trade deficit. In 1960 the return in foreign currency was equivalent to only 20 per cent of the revenue from exports, but it was as much as 35 per cent in 1970—corresponding to 7 per cent of the gross national product, the highest proportion of all European countries.

Factors favouring tourism
Environmental attractions

Summer and winter tourism are, of course, governed by different types of environmental conditions in the high mountains. In summer, water and forests—in winter, snow and sunshine —are the decisive elements as far as attracting tourists is concerned. Winter sports are of greater relative importance at high altitudes in the mountains than are summer holidays.

As can be seen from the diagram of the Salzkammergut area (Fig. 9), there is not only an increase in the duration of sunshine in winter (December, January, February), but there is also a deeper snow cover, lasting much longer. The foehn, however, has a serious effect on winter sports in the Northern Alps (Austria and Bavaria), since it causes snow conditions to be insecure in a large number of winter resorts which happen to enjoy excellent transport connections. The problems faced during the Winter Olympics of 1964 in Innsbruck demonstrate this. Snow had to be carried by lorry from areas protected against the foehn to the Patscherkofel run and the Berg-Isel ski-jump. In areas affected by the foehn the snow usually melts approximately one month earlier in the spring.

There is another climatic factor which has an adverse effect on winter sports, and that is the 'lakes of cold air' (*Kälteseen*) brought about by the diurnal reversal of temperatures in Alpine valleys and basins. Though it makes the snow cover last, it also causes biting frost because the air is very humid. Such areas cannot be recommended for a winter holiday, therefore. Above the 'lakes of cold air', at a height of about 900 to 1000 m, the weather is much more attractive since temperatures are milder.

Forests interfere with skiing and if ski-runs have to be made through them it involves the costly felling of trees; thus, winter sports have

Fig. 9. The relation between certain climatic elements and altitude above sea level, as seen in the Salzkammergut

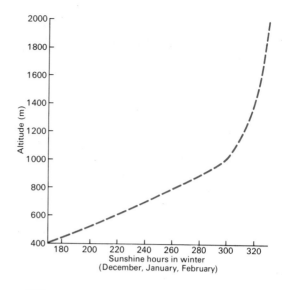

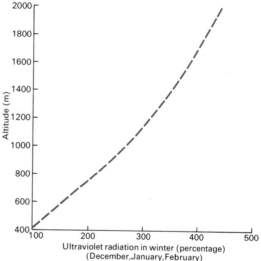

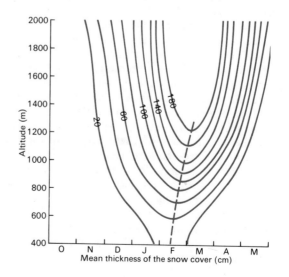

33

their ideal location above the timber-line. The region of Alpine pastures and meadows provides an excellent terrain. Accordingly a winter season is important particularly in those parts of the Eastern Alps which also have extensive summer ranching, such as the greywacke zone between the northern limestone ranges and the Central Alps (Kitzbühel, Arlberg), the high plateaus of the Dolomites, and the high valley of the Engadin (Switzerland). Similar landscapes are encountered in the vicinity of the passes (Seefeld in the Tyrol, Tonale Pass in Southern Tyrol). In the U-shaped valleys, the higher levels, especially the shoulders and the cirques, are being opened up nowadays with the help of cable-cars.

It is clear from the above that the opportunities for skiing in the Eastern Alps can be closely related to an imaginary profile drawn through them from west to east upon which the vertical zoning of vegetation is superimposed. Such a profile would show that the zone of Alpine pastures gets narrower towards the east where it eventually vanishes. There is less opportunity in the forest mountains of the eastern part of the Alps for large-scale development of winter sports than in the west.

A comparable vegetation profile drawn from north to south impressively demonstrates that the highlands of Graubünden and of the Dolomites form a kind of outlier of winter sports, whilst further south the duration of snow cover is much shorter than on the northern side of the Alps, even at higher elevations. The favourable conditions on the northern slope, where a chain of famous resorts with both a summer and a winter season has developed at the foot of the mountains in Bavaria, are related to the considerable precipitation experienced on this windward exposure. Since this falls mainly as winter snow, a blanket of snow several metres thick can form.

The above remarks show that, allowing for natural conditions, a very much smaller area of the Eastern Alps is suitable for winter sports than is for summer tourism. With regard to the latter, the presence of many lake resorts on the southern edges of the Alps and in the Klagenfurt Basin means that tourist traffic spreads extensively into the lower parts of these Alps during the summer. The recreational areas in the vicinity of the large cities catering for their distinctive needs must also be taken into account. It must be noted, however, that the density of tourist traffic is markedly lower in those areas where forests constitute the only recreational attraction, for example the forested mountains of Styria and Lower Austria.

Existing settlements

Tourist traffic affects and is affected by the existing pattern of rural settlement in the mountains. During the earliest phase of tourism it was of the utmost importance for the settlement to be connected by rail and to have an attractive layout, representative architecture, and a good supply of services. Places like Kitzbühel, Zell am See, Meran, and Pörtschach owe their development to these qualities, combined with their mountain setting. Almost totally detached from these resorts in the valleys was the network of mountain refuges which were a response to the growth of mountaineering. The two types of tourist traffic were geographically quite distinct. Only during the inter-war period, when existing rural settlements became modest summer resorts (*Sommerfrische*) was there close contact between the tourist population and the peasants. Such contacts grew as the formerly uneven distribution of tourist traffic was transformed into an almost universal one. More recently winter sports have taken tourist traffic to even higher elevations so that in many places alps have developed into hotel-villages.

Personal factors

Amongst other reasons for the growth of tourism, the initiative of the local population is of crucial importance. It appears that, particularly in the mountainous areas of Switzerland and the Tyrol, enterprising local tradesmen and merchants recognized at an early date the potential to be derived from catering for tourists. In many Tyrolean tourist areas, such as the Ötz valley and around Saalbach in Salzburg, local families in the hotel business have influenced the growth of tourist traffic by organizing the provision of facilities. Sometimes the initiative of just one influential person can transform a not very attractive settlement into a prosperous resort, as was the case, for example, with the mayor of Bad Kleinkirchheim in Upper Carinthia, who succeeded simply by improving the infrastructure of services and by well-planned advertising campaigns. His pioneering efforts are still admired by economic experts.

In contrast with Austria, urban capital played an important role in the growth of tourist traffic in Switzerland, where stock corporations developed large hotel groups. This explains why the hotels frequently stand apart from the old settlements which retain their rural character, as at Davos or St. Moritz. At present attempts are being made, again with urban capital, to expand the tourist trade in the Italian Alps.

Large hotels and many apartment houses are being built.

Buildings

Typical of the earliest phase of tourism are the large hotels, originally urban elements alien to their rural surroundings. In keeping with the architectural tastes of the age, their dimensions and design, as well as their interior decoration and furnishings, were palatial. Individual rooms could be combined to form suites of any size or let separately. The numerous attendants were normally accommodated in the uppermost storeys or in the back premises of the hotel. Parks, golf links, or tennis courts were often incorporated into these hotels.

The grand summer villas set in gardens, and associated especially with the lakes of the Southern Alps (Lake Garda, Lake Como) and the Salzkammergut, with the Carinthian lakes and with resorts of international character such as Kitzbühel, may be considered the earliest forerunners of the second-homes movement.

During the inter-war period the number of newly erected establishments remained small because of the economic depression. In the new

Hotels with characteristic Tyrolean architectural features: Hochgurgl, Ötz Valley, Tyrol (Austria)

summer resorts simple inns and small boarding houses were established, whilst the beginnings of winter sports led to the building of a number of small hotels.

After World War II a new phase of building began with hotels of contrasted styles and character. Up to the late 1960s large hotels were rare, especially in areas where tourism was limited to one season of the year and where, in consequence, returns were least certain. New types of accommodation also appeared. One of these is the so-called hotel garni that is operated with comparatively few employees. Another trend is the growing habit of letting rooms in private houses.

This practice of letting rooms has provided the necessary impetus for further construction activities in the Austrian Alps in which all sections of society are participating. In Switzerland, by contrast, the hotel business has retained its prominence. But the single family house with a 'tourist storey' of rooms for rent is now typical of the settlements in the western Austrian provinces. Here most of the mountain peasants are engaged in tourist activities of one kind or another. General directives have been worked out by the provincial Boards of Works in order to ensure that the traditional house-types do not disappear but are reproduced in standardized form. This is especially the case in the Bavarian, Swiss, and western Austrian Alps, where the architectural features of the Rhaetic *Seitenflurhaus* of the Engadin and the unit-house of Salzburg, the Tyrol, and Upper Bavaria are imitated even in the design of the new hotels, which here cater for two tourist seasons. The position is different, however, in the Italian

Bad Gastein, Salzburg (Austria) as it was in 1871

Southern Alps (with the exception of Southern Tyrol–Trentino). Here second homes, in contrasted architectural styles, predominate. On the one hand the multi-storey rural houses are being adapted, on the other hand huge and incongruous new apartment structures are being added, a form of building brought to the mountains by an urban population used to life in tenement blocks.

Extent of tourism

With regard to tourist traffic today Austria undoubtedly occupies first rank. It offers a million beds for tourists, and about 100 million overnight stays were recorded in 1971/2. Numbers are much lower in the Italian portion of the Eastern Alps. If the lakes and cities on the southern margin are included the number of overnight stays can be estimated at about 40 million. The small Bavarian portion of the Alps—including the Alpine foreland—can boast a total of 25 million (1965/6) and thus surpasses Trentino–Alto Adige, the most visited Italian Alpine province, which recorded about 18 million overnight stays in 1972.

As far as accommodation is concerned, it should be noted that the number of private persons letting rooms to tourists is of considerable importance in Austria. In 1971 about 40 per cent of the overnight stays were accounted for in this way. They now play a vital role in coping with the ever-increasing number of foreign tourists. In addition, they help to overcome the problem arising from the great difference in demand between the summer and the winter seasons. In summer, especially, they provide the extra beds required.

In the other Alpine States, hotels, boarding houses, and inns are of greater relative importance in the provision of tourist accommodation. It is in Switzerland, especially in the Engadin, that hotel-type accommodation is most common. In the Italian Alps, the situation in Southern Tyrol–Trentino comes closest to that in Austria with the emphasis on private letting. The common language and similarities in the way of life with adjacent parts of Austria may explain this. In the rest of the Italian Alps the letting of private rooms during the summer season to visitors from the towns of the Po valley is also of significance. In all about a quarter of the overnight stays in the Italian Alps are accounted for by private rooms.

The concentration problem
Regional concentration
The phenomenon of regional concentration is seen in the fact that many guests spend a large number of nights in comparatively few com-

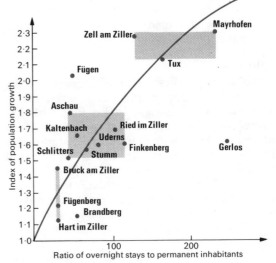

Fig. 10. The relation between population growth and tourism in the Ziller valley, Tyrol

munes. This holds true for all countries, though it is least obvious in Bavaria. In 1971 the share of Austrian communes with more than 200 000 overnight stays accounted for 52·5 per cent of the 88·5 million nights spent in privately-let rooms or hotel-type accommodation. Yet those 106 communes made up only 6·4 per cent of all the 'tourist traffic communes', entitled to collect visitors' tax, and only 4·0 per cent of all Austrian communes. Environmental problems have arisen as a result of the degree of concentration of tourist traffic. Sanitation measures, for example, are being undertaken around a number of lakes at extremely high cost.

Away from these main tourist centres there are large areas of the Alps playing hardly any role in tourism. Prominent amongst these are the lower eastern and south-eastern foothills of the Alps. In the southern forealps, the lack of water and the destruction of the woodland restricts the natural potential of the area for tourism and limits it to altitudes of above 1000 m. Since politicians and planners tend to regard tourism as a means of bringing improvements to under-developed areas, it is hardly surprising that a decentralization of tourist traffic has been called for with increasing frequency over the past ten years. It is, however, much more difficult to reallocate activities involved with tourism than it is to establish new industrial plants when drawing up regional plans. The plan to create 'recreation villages' and the fairly new idea of a 'holiday on the farm', to cater for which special lists are being published in some countries, may be considered an outcome of these intentions. In assessing these efforts one has to bear in mind that certain parts of the Alps will

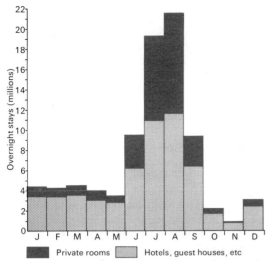

Fig. 11. Seasonal fluctuation in tourism in Austria (1972)

Private rooms ■ Hotels, guest houses, etc ▨

always benefit from their natural advantages. There is also a multiplier effect with regard to the provision of services for the tourist population. At least about 200 000 overnight stays seem to be necessary in order to enable a rural commune to offer an adequate range of services (indoor swimming pools, tennis courts, places of entertainment, etc.).

The effect of tourism as a catalyst to demographic change can be seen in the Ziller valley in the central Austrian Alps. Fig. 10 shows that there is a positive correlation between population growth and the number of overnight stays. The large tourist centres, Mayrhofen and Zell am Ziller, grew most markedly whereas the settlements of medium size exhibited slower growth, about 1·5 to 1·8 per cent, over the same period. The growth rate was slowest in the remote villages, which also had fewest overnight stays.

Thus a degree of regional concentration cannot be avoided where tourism is concerned. There are, however, certain ways by which overconcentration can be avoided. One of these is by the development of satellite centres close to existing tourist nodes. The satellite centres will be less elegant and comfortable, but much cheaper. There the less wealthy and families with young children get a chance to spend their holidays and enjoy some of the advantages of the more fashionable resorts.

In a tourist area with satellite centres one may observe a similar gradient from centre to periphery with regard to price of land, traffic density, number of beds, number of overnight stays, comfort, and prices as can be seen in a town from the C.B.D. towards the suburbs. A tentative

spatial model suggests itself. The following areas can be considered tourist regions of the 'satellite' type: the Arlberg area, the shores of the large Carinthian lakes such as the Wörthersee in Austria, the regions around Cortina d'Ampezzo and Madonna di S. Campiglio in Southern Tyrol, and the area around St. Moritz in the Engadin.

Seasonal concentration
The seasonal concentration of tourist traffic during a very few months of the year is a second basic problem. It is illustrated in Fig. 11, based on Austrian data.

The typical short-term peaks demand a much greater provision of roads and other public facilities than is needed at other times of the year. Another problem, for which no complete solution has yet been found, is that encountered in thousands of hotels and boarding houses during the off-season (Table 7). An extension of the season by 'all-in' offers at bargain prices during the pre- and after-seasons, an intensification of winter sports and short-term recreational activities, are amongst the measures introduced to make better use of the spare capacity.

Concentration by nationality
As we have already seen, the Alpine countries differ with regard to the proportion of native or foreign tourists. Whereas the German Alps are visited almost exclusively by the Germans themselves, the Swiss Alps attract a higher proportion of foreigners. In the Austrian Alps there is a marked contrast between the west and the east: German guests dominate in the west, whilst the east is still sought-after by visitors from the federal capital, Vienna, and the provincial capitals, Linz and Graz. The Italian Alps exhibit a similar pattern. Their northern, more attractive portion (Southern Tyrol) appeals to German tourists, whereas the southern outposts are visited by the town-dwellers of the Po valley.

While 81 per cent of Austria's tourists are foreigners, Southern Tyrol in the Italian Alps has the next highest proportion of foreign tourists with just under 60 per cent. In 1972 Austria

TABLE 7
Percentage of Austrian tourist accommodation utilized (tourist year 1970/71)

November	6·8	May	16·8
December	18·3	June	37·6
January	24·3	July	51·8
February	27·0	August	66·7
March	26·5	September	36·4
April	23·2	October	6·2

Characteristic houses designed for the letting of private rooms: Dienten am Hochkönig, Salzburg (Austria)

Scharnow and Touropa, are deeply involved in the organization of tourism in the Eastern Alps. They have not only entered into agreements with businesses providing accommodation, but they also co-operate with the Austrian Railways. Thus in 1972 the Austrian Railways ran a total of 4967 special trains for tourists, particularly during the summer season.

Peasants and tourists

As industrialization is considered a universal remedy in developing countries, tourist traffic is thought to be a panacea in the areas of mountain peasantry. Thus the old demand for extra sources of income appears in a new guise. In the Bavarian Alps and even more in western Austria and Southern Tyrol, where the mountain peasants live in spacious, solidly built farmsteads, a proportion of the growing number of tourists were accommodated on farms even in the inter-war years. It has become much more common since World War II, and a new phenomenon has emerged—the 'tourist-traffic peasant' (*Fremdenverkehrsbauer*).

Some politicians have realized, to their dismay, that this new, dynamic branch of the economy cannot be controlled as easily as they had thought. The emergence of the 'tourist-traffic peasant' is soon followed by a less desirable feature, the pseudo-rural accommodation enterprise lacking a trade licence. There are serious effects upon agriculture too, for in tourist centres it is deprived of all the labour still available. The home pastures, once in such great demand that there were legal actions over them and boundary-stones were moved by night, are now being left fallow and are no longer mowed (Cortina d'Ampezzo, Seefeld, Arlberg, and the Bavarian Alps). The income derived from tourist traffic discourages the peasant from farming intensively, and he is encouraged to reduce his livestock numbers as the cash return from a well-frequented double-bedded room is comparable with that from one cow. This is the worst side of the picture, however. It cannot be denied that the income derived from tourist traffic, which can be considerable at times, has given thousands of mountain peasants a chance to retain their holdings and to modernize them. Often it has enabled children unable to succeed to a farm to settle on a lot detached from their parents' holding. Thus a diligent and able section of the population is kept from leaving the high mountains. When not engaged in tourism it commutes to the industrialized settlements of the main valleys.

overtook Italy with a total of 72 million overnight stays of foreigners. Because the average length of stay is slightly shorter in Italy (5·4 days, compared with 7), the actual number of foreign tourists is higher in Italy, however.

In 1971 more than 75 per cent of Austria's foreign tourists came from West Germany. A similar proportion can be observed only in Southern Tyrol. In Graubünden the percentage of Germans is less than 50, and it is even smaller in the western Swiss Alps.

The predominance of tourists from West Germany, particularly in western Austria, is due not only to ease of access, but, as in Southern Tyrol, is an outcome of the German language being common to both countries. In the western provinces the menus are adapted to the tastes of the Germans, and the names of the dishes are given in the form the guests are used to. Moreover, the DM has become a sort of second 'national legal tender' that is being accepted almost everywhere.

Because of the large percentage of German tourists the major German travel agencies,

38

The differences between *Almbauern* and *Waldbauern* referred to above are reflected in the degree of involvement in tourist traffic. It is only the peasants in Vorarlberg, the Tyrol, and Salzburg who have so far made a worthwhile profit from letting rooms, whereas fewer than one-fifth of the holdings derive an income from tourism in the eastern, less attractive parts of the Alps. The contribution of tourist traffic towards total income differs correspondingly. It can amount to 30 per cent in western Austria, but is no more than 10 to 15 per cent on average. The rooms in farmsteads are also amongst those occupied for the shortest periods since they do not offer a large measure of comfort.

From the point of view of their increasing importance to winter sports the relationship between tourism and the Alpine pastures deserves special comment. As the chalets on the Alpine pastures are vacant for the greater part of the year, and especially during the skiing season when accommodation is in great demand, it follows that some of them will be leased to visitors. This practice is of greatest importance in the Bavarian Alps. In the so-called Isarwinkel two-thirds of all dairy huts were already being let to tourists by 1965. A similar integration of the economy of the alps and tourism has not been attained throughout the Eastern Alps, however. In western Tyrol, for example, only 25 per cent of the alps yield an income from tourist traffic.

In Austria the growth of winter sports has caused modest alp settlements to become well-known tourist centres. Examples are Hochkrummbach in the Arlberg region of Vorarlberg, Hochgurgl and Kühtai in the Ötztal Alps, Hintertux in the Tux Alps of the Tyrol, and Obertauern in the Niedere Tauern of Salzburg. A certain amount of statistical information is available for these areas. Some years ago there were only 17 chalets in the Zürs area, now there are 5 hotels and 11 'hotels garni'. More than 100 000 nights are spent there by tourists, yielding the equivalent of 20 million AS in foreign exchange. The Alpine pastures, carefully cultivated over a long period, have played an important role in this remarkable development, affording a great many ski-runs of varying difficulty and length, and having an ample snow cover for about 200 days of the year. It might be noted that there are still 60 dairy cows and 170 other head of cattle grazed there in summer. On the Alpine pastures of Obertauern there was little accommodation offered some 40 years ago. At present there are 3000 tourist beds, and the 22 cable-railways and ski-lifts can transport 18 000 people an hour.

There are several examples of the integrated development of Alpine pastures, including the 'skiing circuses' of the Arlberg area and Kitzbühel where 24 and 29 mechanical devices respectively are available for the ascent (Fig. 12). As the alps are opened up, the importance of ski runs below the timber-line is decreasing in favour of those above it. The role of the Alpine pastures for winter sports can be deduced from the fact that in Austria, half of the 14 cable-railways and all six chair-lifts constructed in 1969 take people up to this region.

Public aid for tourism

Austria may again serve as an example of how tourism is promoted in the mountains. Since World War II there have been four phases, each with its particular objective.

1. Immediately after the War there was much leeway to make up in the provision of infrastructure. Improvements to the road network and the construction of cable-railways, chair-lifts, and ski-lifts thus had priority in the development programme.

2. An attempt was next made to open up new tourist areas. Subsidies were granted to local authorities and to tourist associations, and funds were made available for new accommodation. Another aim was to prolong the tourist season by providing outdoor swimming pools, by marking footpaths, and by the improvement of facilities generally.

3. From about 1965 emphasis shifted to improvements in the standard of accommodation (installation of running water, toilets, showers, central heating, modern catering equipment, etc.). An increase in the number of beds available was the object only in development areas. An attempt was also made to co-ordinate the plans and activities of individual tourist organizations and to start advertising campaigns.

4. Improvements to accommodation have

Fig. 12. The Kitzbühel 'skiing circus'

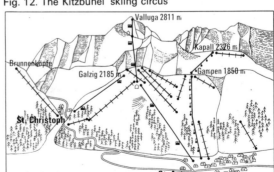

continued to be made since 1969 but, in addition, projects aimed at increasing the general attractiveness of the country for tourists have also got under way (bypasses, installations for heating the water in open-air swimming baths, indoor swimming baths, construction of buildings for spare-time activities, tourist information services, preservation of historic buildings, and organization of cultural events). In the winter sports areas, attention has been directed to the improvement and upkeep of ski-runs. Facilities for the supply of drinking water and of sewage disposal have been improved. In 1972 the Austrian provinces as a whole earmarked about 300 million AS in their budgets for the purposes of promoting tourism.

Problems posed by tourism
Natural hazards

Catastrophes, such as mountain torrents and avalanches, are typical hazards in the high mountains. In past centuries it was usually possible to avoid the danger zones since the density of settlement was low and the exposed sites were well-known. Even when the little-frequented roads became impassable for several weeks it did not greatly matter. The rapid growth of tourism, however, has resulted in building taking place in those areas that are subject to natural hazards.

Tyrol can serve as an example for studying the extent of this problem. Here there are something like 620 mountain torrents and 1100 avalanches that can constitute a threat to the settlements or to the maintenance of traffic routes in winter. The sum needed for efficient control measures is said to be 2·3 thousand million AS, but only 70 million AS a year can be made available for this purpose. It would thus take a generation's work to ensure the complete safety of the settlements and traffic routes as they now exist. It seems to be absolutely necessary to reserve larger public funds for torrent- and avalanche-control, but measures must also be taken to prevent unplanned developments that ignore the natural conditions and add still more to the cost of protection.

Management problems

Since the Eastern Alps are a highly dynamic tourist area, supply has to adapt not only to an increasing number of tourists but still more to their steadily rising demands for comfort. Many facilities more than ten years old must, therefore, be considered out-of-date. This is particularly true in those areas receiving large numbers of foreigners who require a higher standard of

Structures providing protection against avalanches on the Arlberg Road between the Tyrol and Vorarlberg (Austria)

comfort than do Austrian tourists. Whilst rooms with the normal hot and cold running water can still be offered in the tourist centres of eastern Austria frequented by Austrian nationals, there is a growing demand for rooms with private baths and showers in western Austria, and the older forms of accommodation are forced to adapt to this need.

Taking into account the potential of other parts of the Continent we must not overlook the fact that the Alps have to face increasing competition from the Mediterranean region. Tourist areas outside Europe are also gaining in importance. There is, however, no other economic activity in which it is so difficult to anticipate possible future changes in demand as in tourism, depending as it does to such a large extent on changes of fashion. It is perhaps remarkable that in spite of the enormous significance of tourism to the Alpine economy, small enterprises still predominate in almost all places.

In addition to basic problems relating to the low return on capital caused by the short season, there are increasing difficulties in the labour market nowadays. Jobs in tourism are not the most attractive ones in those Alpine countries faced with over-employment (Germany, Austria, and Switzerland). It is only the best positions in first-class hotels that are attractive enough to be filled with skilled personnel from the big cities. A mass of unskilled immigrant labour has therefore had to be recruited. The quality of service during the height of the season is not improved, yet the enterprises could not be managed without these foreign workers, at present mainly Yugoslavs and Turks. In the Italian Alps it is, however, possible to employ seasonal workers drawn predominantly from southern Italy.

Social problems

The physical effects of tourism upon existing settlements can be compared with those resulting from the industrialization of the towns in the 1870s. In the areas affected there are rapid changes as new building takes place that is frequently not in harmony with its surroundings. Admittedly there are building regulations which result in some standardization of new house types, at least within a single province. Unfortunately, imaginative new designs appropriate for tourist centres are rare, and ideas for their successful integration into the existing settlements are also lacking. Tourist settlements remain a stronghold of speculation in real estate, in contrast with the planning control that is now exercised in towns. In the tourist centres of the Alps, an area offering only limited space for settlement, real estate prices have reached heights eclipsing even those associated with the central business districts of large cities.

In view of this it is hardly surprising that high-rise buildings are mushrooming in the most popular recreation areas of the Eastern Alps. At the same time there is growing opposition to such projects, most vocal in the German-speaking areas. Radio Austria, in fact, broadcasts a weekly satirical programme, 'Reports from the Culture Front', which regularly criticizes the building of apartment blocks in the attractive recreation areas of Austria. The extravagant project of a Stuttgart construction company, 'Meran 2000', enraged the public in Southern Tyrol for many months. Eventually the plan, involving a skyscraper apartment-hotel (120 m high, 34 storeys, 1000 beds) being built above Meran at an altitude of 1900 m, was dropped.

The Meran project serves to introduce a second, and related, problem: the growing tendency for an urban population to acquire second homes in a rural setting. In the Austrian, the Swiss, and portions of the Italian Alps this problem is aggravated by the fact that the parties concerned are mainly foreigners, principally citizens of West Germany, who are much better off financially than the local population. An indication of the size of this problem is the fact that half of the lots on the shores of most of the Salzkammergut lakes, as well as those in Tyrolean settlements such as Seefeld, are owned by foreigners.

The pressure put on the authorities by public opinion fearing the development of a German 'pensionopolis' in the western Austrian Alps has resulted in stricter regulations governing the sale of real estate in Vorarlberg, the Tyrol, and Salzburg, making it difficult for foreigners to become landowners. The building of summer houses has now almost stopped in the west, but there are still apartment blocks under construction. In the future there will be fewer of these, since it recently became necessary to obtain a special permit to build high-rise structures. Because of these legal regulations in the west, the wave of apartment-house building for Germans is now speading to Upper Austria, especially to the Salzkammergut. The scale of the development becomes obvious from daily newspaper reports that in spring 1972 there were no fewer than 7000 apartment units being built in the Salzkammergut and that there would be 1000 apartments added to the already existing ones in Bad Ischl.

The building of second homes for foreigners closely follows the distribution of visitors during the summer season, being most extensive in the attractive tourist areas. Where once the second homes were found mainly in the vicinity of large cities, now they have spread to the more remote parts of the country.

The problems posed by second homes are of various kinds. Often such homes are being built without sufficient planning and sometimes they are too numerous to be supported by the existing local services. Dispersed homesteads, especially new ones, may impair the aesthetic qualities of the landscape. Access to certain areas is being restricted, particularly when the shores of lakes are being built upon.

If the proportion of second houses gets too high, there is a danger that the resident population will have to live in some sort of 'ghost town' for the greater part of the year. The rising price of real estate and an increasing shortage of land render communal projects, such as sports grounds, car parks, etc., more difficult to achieve. The local authorities are also faced with the cost of adding to the road network, drainage facilities, and water supply. In return they gain only periodic inhabitants who do not contribute to the local tax income.

Perspectives of mass tourism

Mass tourism can be divided into two broad categories: first, the tourism typical of the summer and winter seasons; and secondly, the recreational activities of the large city populations. These forms have different requirements with regard to the physical qualities of the environment, access, and the type and nature of the accommodation and other facilities. Recreation for city dwellers involves easy access, inns and restaurants, sports grounds, and various entertainment facilities, including sites to be visited. By contrast, seasonal tourists normally intend to stay for longer periods and, therefore, make quite different demands with regard to the accommodation. Facilities must be provided for periods of both good and bad weather (tennis courts, golf links, indoor swimming baths, cinemas, night-clubs, etc.). Local services must reach a certain standard. The higher demands of foreign tourists for services and comfort were considered in an earlier chapter.

Summer and winter visitors

On a Continental scale, European tourists generally move from north to south, from the highly industrialized countries, such as the Benelux States, West Germany, and the United Kingdom, towards the sun or snow further south. National boundaries introduce a degree of friction affecting this movement and the tourist build-up can be seen, for example, at the border between Bavaria and Austria. The number of overnight stays recorded at Bavarian settlements in the Alps

displays a balance between the summer and winter seasons hardly ever reached by Austrian tourist centres. In Germany the main tourist centres are situated at the foot of the Alps, whereas there are two distinct types of location in Austria. On the one hand, a row of old tourist centres is situated along the railway which follows the valleys. Places such as Kitzbühel, Zell am See, and Bischofshofen have become the foci of intensively visited tourist areas. On the other hand, skiing has caused tourism to invade the zone of the high Alps just below the snow-line, where new winter sports centres have come into existence.

In the Italian and Swiss portions of the Eastern Alps it is only the higher portions, such as the Engadin in Switzerland and the high Dolomites in Southern Tyrol, that have attained the status of truly international tourist regions. Tourist centres at the foot of the northern Alps attract visitors in summer and winter. Similar conditions can be observed to a limited degree in the Carinthian lake region, but the double season is missing completely on the Italian southern slope of the Alps because of climatic reasons. In the Italian forealps winter sports are of purely local importance (Sette Communi, Val Trompia in the Bergamasc Alps—each with only a very few chair-lifts and ski-lifts).

In a schematic profile from north to south along the meridian of Innsbruck (Fig. 13) an attempt has been made to represent the altitudinal limits of summer holiday resorts and winter sports areas, each in turn related to climatic conditions. In the Austrian Alps it is still possible to involve the settlements in the valleys in winter sports activities by the use of

Fig. 13. A profile through the Eastern Alps from north to south showing the seasonal nature of tourism

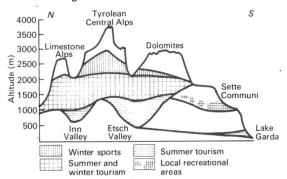

Fig. 14. The decreasing intensity of tourism in Austria from west to east

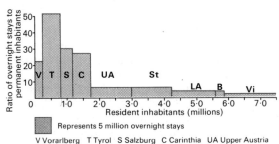

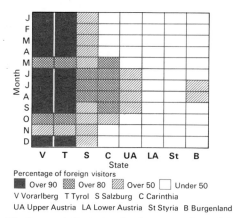

Fig. 15. Seasonal fluctuation in the proportion of foreign tourists in Austria (1972)

Percentage of foreign visitors
■ Over 90 ▨ Over 80 ▨ Over 50 □ Under 50
V Vorarlberg T Tyrol S Salzburg C Carinthia
UA Upper Austria LA Lower Austria St Styria B Burgenland

cable-cars. Kitzbühel provides an excellent example. In the Southern Alps there is, however, an altitudinal zone without any tourism. It extends from just above the Insubrian lake region up to about 800 or 1000 m above sea level. Tiny mountain villages, greatly dilapidated until quite recently, are now being transformed into country retreats for the cities in the valleys and at the foot of the Alps.

A profile through the Austrian Alps from west to east (Fig. 14) differs from that from north to south, as may be expected. If the number of overnight stays per inhabitant is taken as a measure of the intensity of tourist traffic, the Tyrol represents the maximum with 52 overnight stays per inhabitant and there is a sharp decline towards the eastern slope of the Alps in Burgenland with only 3 overnight stays.

Table 8 illustrates the traditional attraction of the western high Alps of Austria as well as the fact that the stream of tourists from West Germany

enters the country from the west. The sharp decline in the intensity of tourist traffic towards Upper Austria and Styria coincides with a diminution in the percentage of foreign tourists. Historical evidence exhibits a steady advance of foreign visitors in search of new attractive areas. Whereas the Carinthian lakes were still the preserve of Austrian, mainly Viennese, tourists during the inter-war period, as were most of the Salzkammergut lakes as late as the 1960s, there is a majority of well-to-do foreigners in both of these areas now.

The diffusion of tourist traffic is most noticeable in the summer season (Fig. 15), during which foreign visitors have recently become the majority in Burgenland. There is thus an increasing pressure on the Austrians who are compelled by rising prices to visit inexpensive foreign countries, such as Yugoslavia and Italy, or to go to little-developed summer resorts in the forested mountains of Lower Austria and Styria.

This pressure on native tourists to seek out the less attractive areas is common to both the Austrian and the Italian Alps. In the latter area, the tide of foreign tourists is expanding in several directions, from Southern Tyrol eastwards towards the Fella valley and to the west as far as the Tonale Pass.

Recreation for city-dwellers
Recreational travel on the part of the city-dwellers of the forelands differs from the pattern described above, both with regard to the distances covered and to the degree of investment in second homes. The size of city and the wealth of its inhabitants are both important considerations.

Munich, the dynamic capital of Bavaria,

TABLE 8

Overnight stays and intensity of tourism in the Austrian provinces (1972)

	Total	Overnight stays foreigners (thousands)	Foreigners (per cent)	Overnight stays per 100 inhabitants
Tyrol	28 291	26 625	95	5 232
Salzburg	15 715	12 510	79	3 911
Carinthia	14 318	11 948	85	2 703
Vorarlberg	5 752	5 297	92	2 119
Styria	7 579	2 542	33	636
Upper Austria	7 360	4 111	55	602
Lower Austria	5 318	1 051	20	376
Burgenland	905	382	42	333
Vienna	3 358	2 935	87	208
Austria (excluding public sanatoria)	88 596	67 401	76	1 187

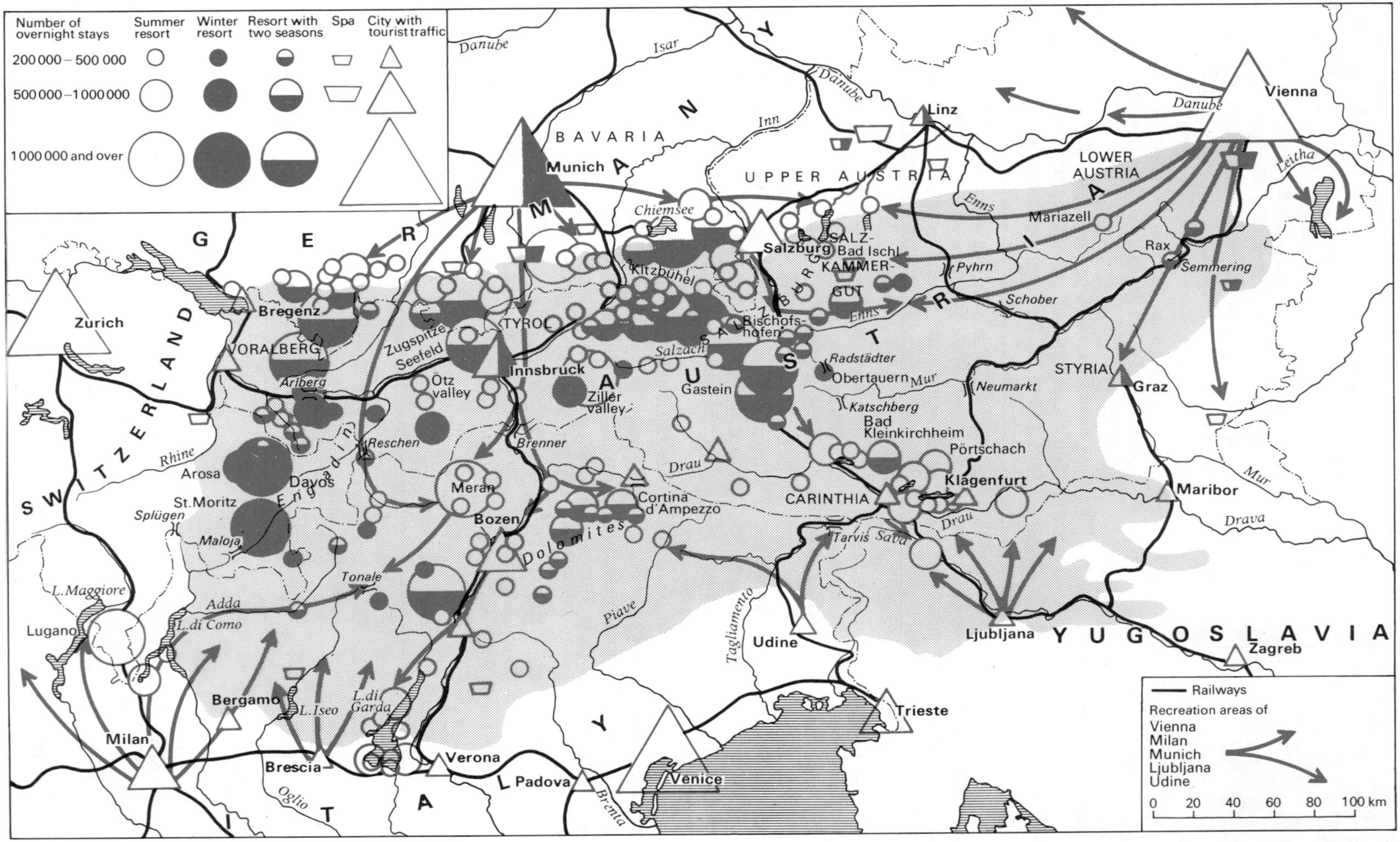

Map 4. Tourism and recreation areas in the Eastern Alps, 1971/72.

44

generates the largest number of tourists. The flow of tourists from Munich reaches not only the Bavarian Alps, but also large parts of the Tyrol and Vorarlberg and even Southern Tyrol. It is not unusual for active young people fond of winter sports to drive to and from the Dolomites for a weekend. The urge to build second homes in these places is thus a strong one. The resulting problems have been discussed above.

The Austrian capital, Vienna, has access to a great variety of recreation areas in Lower Austria and in the northern part of Burgenland. In summer, however, Viennese visitors are in the majority only in Lower Austria. In the Steirisches Randgebirge and in the Mürz valley the recreational hinterlands of Vienna and Graz appear to be superimposed. The same is true of part of the Styrian limestone Alps, especially in winter since winter-sports movement traditionally involves longer distances because in the area around Vienna the demand for ski-lifts and runs is much larger than the supply. In the high Alps the weekend visitors from German towns can enjoy the well-developed facilities provided for winter-sports tourists. Within the recreational hinterlands of Graz and Linz—extending towards the Mühlviertel in the north and towards the Salzkammergut in the south—the building of second homes is as yet of limited importance, whereas construction is remarkably active in the Vienna region and has brought about fundamental changes in the settlement pattern.

The larger Italian cities also satisfy their recreational needs in the Alps. Milan, the economic capital of Italy, looks mainly towards Lake Como, where, for example, huge apartment blocks have been built in the Maggio area. In contrast with Milan, recreational movement in the hinterlands of Brescia and Bergamo has not had much influence on the settlement pattern. Likewise in the small recreational area serving the capital of Slovenia, Ljubljana, which extends towards the Karawanken, only a few exclusive summer houses have appeared at high altitudes in the north of the Ljubljana Basin.

The areas of mountain peasantry

In seeking to distinguish one area of mountain peasantry from another, one must now take into account, not only the changes brought about by the spread of commuting, but also the impact of tourism in its several forms. The older differences, described in earlier chapters, have been partly veiled by these new developments.

The northern limestone ranges, generally speaking, have always been a zone of limited agricultural potential. Farming was limited to the transverse valleys, passes, and flatter portions of the mountain slopes. Large forest estates, in many cases former possessions of the Crown but now public property, have led the way in the introduction of well-planned forest management. Tourism is most common where valley glaciers reached the Alpine foreland during the Ice Age, leaving terminal basins now occupied by lakes. This is most true of the German part of the Alps and the Salzkammergut in Austria. There tourism has resulted in the rural appearance of the settlements vanishing almost completely and the agriculture losing all importance. As we have seen, game are more common than cattle in the Bavarian Alps. Only in the eastern limestone ranges of Upper and Lower Austria does scattered rural settlement still predominate. Though this latter region has become part of the recreation hinterland of Linz and Vienna, there have been no profound changes as yet.

The contrast between east and west is even more marked in the Central Alps than in the northern limestone ranges. The economic and social differences between the *Almbauern* in the west and the *Waldbauern* in the east were considered in some detail above. These distinctions have been increased by the effects of tourism.

Thus tourism has attained its greatest intensity in those mountains of the Eastern Alps in which rural settlement has also reached the very highest elevations, in Graubünden (Switzerland) and the Tyrolean Central Alps, where foreigners account for the majority of the visitors. The settlements have been enlarged and consolidated despite the trend towards a less intensive agriculture, the abandonment of crop farming, and a decline in livestock numbers. Commuting to the small and medium-sized industrial units of the Tyrolean Inn valley, most of which have been founded since World War II, has also contributed to the further growth of the settlements. As a result the Tyrol now has a population density in the settled areas that is equal to that of the Netherlands (370 persons per sq. km). Traditional farmhouses have served as a model for the many new single-family houses, especially with regard to the shape of the roof, the balconies, and the painting, and the style has been imitated to some extent in the design of hotels also.

As a result of geological structure, the southern slope of the Alps in Italy (Southern Tyrol, Valtellino) is much steeper. Furthermore, the Italian Government has shown less initiative in the development of the Alpine regions. Thus conditions are less attractive to tourists there,

The spreading of apartment houses in the Italian Southern Alps: Moggio, east of Lake Como

and in consequence there are still serious losses of population towards the upper limit of settlement (Brenta, Ortler, Adamello districts).

The lowering of the Central Alps towards the east brings about a change in landforms and in land use. There are only a few cirques dissecting the ridges in central Carinthia and in Styria, offering physical features less attractive to tourists than those in the western high Alps. The peasants, dependent on their forests, are not able to participate in tourism to the same extent as those in the western high Alps. Reference has already been made to the changes affecting agriculture and the problem of constructing access roads in this highly dissected country, where the farmsteads are situated, one above the other, on the divides between the valleys. The eastern part, the Steirisches Randgebirge and its foothills, con-

stitutes the recreation area for Graz and, to some extent, for Vienna.

Of all of the southern limestone ranges only the highland area of the Dolomites has been able to attract international tourist traffic. *Sozialbrache* (non-productive agricultural land) is therefore widespread in the Dolomites, because of the dominant position of tourism. This accounts for the various protective measures taken by the Italian Government. The recent extension of tourism into the basin of the Cadore, which possesses similar physical features, and towards the Tagliamento valley in the east and the Tonale Pass in the west, has been mentioned above. Apart from this development, large areas of the Italian southern limestone ranges must be considered a region of decline, though some life is returning here and there where people spend summer holidays or come on weekend trips. It is in the settlements at more than 1000 m above sea level that revival of this kind is most evident. The amount of land under cultivation is still contracting, however, particularly in the terraced areas. Only in those regions where a grassland economy and cattle farming are traditional (Sette Communi, Val Trompia) does agricultural production survive, partly in the form of co-operatives. The zone lacking tourist traffic (Fig. 13) more or less corresponds with one of declining settlement, sandwiched between the areas of intensive cultivation (vineyards and orchards) in the Alpine foothills and a few valleys (Valtellino), and the higher zone of cattle breeding and grassland economy.

Strategy for the future

Recently the public has become more aware of the role of the Alps as a recreation area for the highly industrialized European countries. It is all the more surprising, therefore, that there should still be considerable ignorance, of both the problems and the possibilities involved in the further development of the Alpine region. A number of observations may be made in conclusion.

Different environmental conditions are encountered, not only between the northern and the southern Alps, but also between the western high Alps and the lower eastern spurs. Thus the possibilities, whether they be for agriculture or forestry, for tourism, or for the utilization of water-power, vary spatially as well as over the course of time.

The Alps occupy a quite different geographical location within individual countries. As far as Austria and Switzerland are concerned, the

Eastern Alps constitute central problem regions, whereas they are only marginal ones in Germany and Italy.

The Alps must also be regarded as parts of different political and economic systems. Consequently different policies apply, for example, to the production and marketing of agricultural products as well as to tourism.

The latter distinctions are also important with regard to the labour market. Thus Germany, offering higher wages, attracts labour from the neighbouring Austrian provinces, mainly because of the great demand in the Munich region. There is a similar relationship between Austria and Switzerland. A large number of workers living in Austrian Vorarlberg commute daily to Switzerland.

Decisions concerning the future of the Alps are often taken by authorities outside the region. Thus, for example, the network of long-distance routes between one country and another is likely to be worked out in Vienna, Bonn, Rome, or Berne. Agriculture and forestry depend on decisions made by committees of the E.E.C. in Brussels.

It is hardly surprising that no priorities have been agreed upon as to the future of the Alpine region, even whether it is to be viewed solely as a recreational area or whether a multi-functional use is to be aimed at. Tourism as an economic activity is highly susceptible to crises. This explains why a country like Austria, badly hit by the 1000 DM regulation of the 1930s, must advocate diversification. But if the use of the mountains is to be multi-functional, where should the emphasis be placed?

Decisions are made not only at a national level, but also at a provincial and a local one. Both the provinces and the communes are entitled to play a role and to take decisions on certain matters. The significance of provincial boundaries has been pointed out in connection with Southern Tyrol-Trentino. Similar problems arise because of different legal regulations, for example with regard to the real estate market, to building regulations, and to measures governing tourism generally.

In addition to recognizing the great political power exercised by provinces within States that are organized on a federal basis (West Germany, Austria, Switzerland), it must be noted that communes are still the basic political and administrative units in all of the Alpine States and that their points of view must be taken into account in connection with all decisions made at a higher administrative level.

In conclusion it must be stressed that, in spite of a general readiness on the part of the Alpine States to co-operate multilaterally, there are still a great many considerations that prevent them reaching an agreement on the future of the Alps as a whole. Even within individual countries the various 'Alpine Plans' are still under discussion and will not come into force in the near future. The present situation is, therefore, characterized by a wide range of individual measures carried out by a multitude of well-intentioned local authorities, organizations, and private individuals. As to regional planning and multilateral co-operation, there is still a long way to go before some sort of general consensus can be reached relating to all aspects of life and the economy.

Further Work

There is no study in English that adequately covers the regional geography of the Eastern Alps.

The standard work on this subject is still considered to be:

KREBS, N., *Die Ostalpen und das heutige Österreich*, two volumes (J. Engelhorn, Stuttgart, 1928).

Recently a comprehensive study on the Alps was published in French:

VEYRET, P. and G., *Au coeur de l'Europe : les Alpes* (Flammarion, Paris, 1967).

As to the Swiss Alps, the following book can be recommended:

GUTERSOHN, H., *Geographie der Schweiz*, Vol. II, Parts 1 and 2 (Kümmerly & Frey, Berne, 1964).

Fundamental research into the problem of mountain peasantry is to be found in the following:

FRÖDIN, G., *Zentraleuropas Alpwirtschaft* (Oslo, 1940/1). This is the only synopsis of alpine economy published to date.

GORFER, A., *Erben der Einsamkeit* (Trient, 1973).

HARTKE, W. and RUPPERT, K. (eds.), *Almgeographie* (Steiner, Wiesbaden, 1964).

Istituto Nazionale di Economia Agrara, *Lo spopolamento montano in Italia* (Rome, 1932). This is the first and, to date, the most complete study of all the mountainous areas of Italy, including the Italian Alps. Although it is now of mainly historical interest, it gives a detailed account of depopulation and its economic consequences for agriculture.

LICHTENBERGER, E., 'Das Bergbauernproblem in den österreichischen Alpen. Perioden und Typen der Entsiedlung', *Erdkunde,* **19** (1965), p. 39.

LÖHR, L., *Bergbauernwirtschaft im Alpenraum* (Stock, Graz, 1971). This is a highly instructive synopsis from the point of view of economic management.

RUPPERT, K., DEURINGER, L., and MAIER, J., *Das Bergbauerngebiet der deutschen Alpen*, WGI–Berichte zur Regionalforschung 7 (University of Munich, 1971).

The following are excellent monographs:

Almgeographische Studien in den slowenischen Alpen, Münchner Studien zur Sozial- und Wirtschaftsgeographie 5 (Regensburg, 1969).

DÖHRMANN, W., *Bonitierung und Tragfähigkeit eines Alpentales. Innerstes Defereggen in Osttirol,* Westfälische Geographische Studien 24 (Münster, 1972).

HERBIN, J., 'L'insertion du tourisme dans la haute montagne: l'example de Tux dans les Alpes du Zillertal (Tyrol autrichien)', *Revue de géographie alpine,* **57** (1969), p. 665.

PICARD, A., *Les vallées septentrionales du massif de l'Oetztal* (S.E.D.E.S., Paris, 1963).

Although no synoptic studies on the problem of tourist traffic in the Eastern Alps have yet been published, some excellent monographs are:

FREI, H., 'Der Fremdenverkehr in seiner Bedeutung für die Bergbevölkerung am Beispiel Damüls im Bregenzer Wald', *Mitteilungen der Geographischen Gesellschaft München,* **55** (1970), p. 135.

GRÖTZBACH, E., 'Die Entwicklung der bayerischen Fremdenverkehrsgebiete in den letzten vierzig Jahren', *Mitteilungen der Geographische Gesellschaft München,* **53** (1968), p. 262.

JÜLG, F., *Die Seilbahnen Österreichs und ihre Auswirkungen auf die Wirtschaft*, Veröffentlichungen des Österreichischen Instituts für Raumplanung 29 (Vienna, 1966).

MAIER, J., *Die Leistungskraft einer Fremdenverkehrsgemeinde—Modellanalyse des Marktes Hindelang, Allgäu*, WGI–Berichte zur Regionalforschung 3 (University of Munich, 1970).

PEVETZ, W., *Die Beziehungen zwischen Fremdenverkehr, Landwirtschaft und Bauerntum unter besonderer Berücksichtigung der österreichischen Verhältnisse* (Vienna, 1966).

RISCH, P., 'Rückblick und Ausblick im schweizerischen Fremdenverkehr', *Wirtschafts- und Finanzbulletin der Kantonalbank von Bern* (1966).

ROSA, D., *Der Einfluss des Fremdenverkehrs auf ausgewählte Branchen des tertiären Sektors im bayrischen Alpenvorland*, WGI–Berichte zur Regionalforschung 2 (University of Munich, 1970).

Studies pertaining to regional planning are:

DANZ, W., *Aspekte einer Raumordnung in den Alpen*, WGI–Berichte zur Regionalforschung 1 (University of Munich, 1970).

WICHMANN, H. (ed.), *Die Zukunft der Alpenregion?* (Carl Hanser, Munich, 1972).